The Shape of the Past

The Shape of the Past

Gordon Graham

Oxford   New York

OXFORD UNIVERSITY PRESS

1997

Oxford University Press, Great Clarendon Street, Oxford OX2 6DP

Oxford New York
Athens Auckland Bangkok Bombay Buenos Aires
Calcutta Cape Town Dar es Salaam Delhi
Florence Hong Kong Istanbul Karachi
Kuala Lumpur Madras Madrid Melbourne
Mexico City Nairobi Paris Singapore
Taipei Tokyo Toronto
and associated companies in
Berlin Ibadan

Oxford is a trade mark of Oxford University Press

British Library Cataloguing in Publication Data
Data available

Library of Congress Cataloging in Publication Data
Data available

ISBN 019-289255-X

10 9 8 7 6 5 4 3 2 1

Typeset by Graphicraft Typesetters Ltd., Hong Kong
Printed in Great Britain
on acid-free paper by
Biddles Ltd.
Guildford & King's Lynn

In memory of my father,
to whom I owe my sense of history

Acknowledgements

I BEGAN thinking about the topics in this book almost as soon as I discovered what philosophy was, and I first outlined its contents in my mind about ten years ago. Throughout this period I have learnt enormously from teachers, colleagues and students in the universities of St Andrews and Durham. In particular, I have had the opportunity to formulate many of the ideas and arguments the book contains, by an almost continuous, and somewhat unusual, obligation to teach both philosophy of religion and political theory at honours and graduate level. For this opportunity and to the people involved I am very grateful. But my greatest intellectual debt is undoubtedly to the philosophical stimulus I have been given over many years by the writings of Alasdair MacIntyre and the late Michael Oakeshott. I also owe special thanks to Daniel Rashid for reading the whole typescript and alerting me to many typographical, literary and historical as well as philosophical mistakes. It would be hard to find a more widely read critic.

Parts of Chapters 3 and 4 first appeared in *Philosophy* and I gladly acknowledge permission to include them here.

Contents

1 Giving the Past a Shape

Is there a logic of history? Is there, beyond all the causal and incalculable elements of the separate events, something that we may call a metaphysical structure of historic humanity, something that is essentially independent of the outward forms—social, spiritual and political—which we see so clearly? Are not these actualities indeed secondary or derived from that something? Does world-history present to the seeing eye certain grand traits, again and again, with sufficient constancy to justify certain conclusions? And if so, what are the limits to which reasoning from such premises may be pushed? (Spengler, p. 3. Full details of works cited will be found in the Bibliography.)

So writes Oswald Spengler at the start of his monumental book *The Decline of the West*, and it is with these questions, or some of them, that this much shorter book is concerned.

Spengler thinks that the sort of interest in history that he proposes to take is novel, and to be contrasted with an interest in the 'elements of separate events'. We might be led to think by this that hitherto (i.e. before Spengler) all history was concerned with the mere recording of what actually happened. In fact the desire to have a knowledge of the past entirely for its own sake and without practical or theoretical aims is a relatively sophisticated, and for the most part relatively recent, intellectual endeavour. Historical writing from most periods is characterized by a less detached view of the past. Indeed, it is arguable that all cultures that lend importance to an awareness of their own past will inevitably generate a literature (or oral tradition of story-telling) which aims to ascertain within history some hidden meaning—cosmic significance, general direction or providential purpose perhaps. These different 'meanings' are not the same—a direction need not imply a purpose—but they have generally been sought with the same aim: to cast light upon present events and speculate successfully upon the future.

Broadly speaking, interest in the past of this practical sort has predominated over a more academic concern, the study of what has sometimes been called 'scientific history', the sort of study that modern historians generally engage in. By 'scientific history' is here meant the attempt simply to arrive at an accurate account of past events based upon sufficient evidence, without regard to learning lessons, predicting the future course of events, or grasping the 'meaning' of human history as a whole. To say that a practical interest in the past has overshadowed a more academic one is not to deny that traces of a concern with scientific history can be found in the ancient world; there is reason to regard Herodotus (484–?424 BC) as one of its earliest and in some ways finest practitioners, for instance, and it was *detachment* from ultimate meaning that led Augustine (AD 354–430) to regard the 'pagan' history of his own time as seriously inadequate. But much more prominently, and even earlier, in the cultures of which the Western world is the contemporary inheritor, we find a broader, more ambitious endeavour which might be described as the attempt to look beneath the surface of events and find their inner or ultimate significance.

The most familiar histories of this kind have been religious. A marked feature of Judaism, for instance, perhaps indeed its most striking characteristic, is a belief in the revelatory power of the past to disclose, and to confirm, a relationship between a people and their God. The Jewish religion, as its sacred books reveal, is coloured in large part by the desire to formulate a sacred history. At almost every turn the writers of the Old Testament try to move behind such historical events as the exodus from Egypt or the removal of the Jews to Babylon and detect in them the purposes of God. Very many of the books of the Old Testament display this search for a transcendent historical meaning. In Isaiah, for instance (which is generally agreed to be the work of at least two authors) a large part of the first prophet's religious purpose is to reveal the conquests, invasions and natural disasters to which Judaea was subjected at one point in its history, as the actions of a God highly displeased by the moral and religious waywardness of his chosen people and unmoved by the ritualistic sacrifices they made it their practice to offer. Isaiah is not peculiar in this respect. The same concern reveals itself again and again in other books and authors.

Jewish theology is sacred history *par excellence*, but in this it is not unique. It has provided, in fact, a model of thinking about the past upon which other religions have sought to improve. Most obviously this is true of Christianity, which advances an alternative sacred history by which a set of events is picked out of the general flow of the past in order to provide the reference points around which a story of divine intentions may be told. This set of events includes many of those from Jewish history, but to these Christianity makes the crucial addition of the Incarnation of God in Jesus, an historical figure of first-century Palestine, through whose life and teaching God can be seen to act directly in historical time. As we shall see in Chapter 7, amongst the Church Fathers it is St Augustine who first makes Christian sacred history most explicit; indeed we owe the term 'sacred history' to him. But much of the general idea is present in the earliest Christian writings, which make extensive use of historical typology, notably that of patriarch, prophet and messiah. For the most part Augustine just draws out this implicit dimension of Christian theology and extends its application to the major events of his own era, especially the final collapse of the Roman empire.

The idea of a 'sacred history' has its origins in these two

religions, and their prominence in Western culture has made its conceptions highly influential in the subsequent development of historical and cultural self-understanding. But the inclusion of the term 'sacred' should not mislead us into thinking that histories of this rather grand sort must always be concerned with the purposes of God, or even, indeed, with the invocation of supernatural agencies. Subsequent, secular, thinkers have taken up the ambition of sacred history and transformed it in essentially non-religious ways. G. W. F. Hegel (1770–1831) may be seen as pivotal in this transformation. Though Hegel believed himself to be providing a rational exposition of the truths obscurely contained in Christianity, the outcome of his reflections on what he called 'world' history was one in which theological categories were in effect systematically replaced by philosophical conceptions. Thus the work of divine agency in Hegel is converted into the activity of 'Reason' itself, and the end of history is not the Kingdom of God but the manifestation of Absolute Mind or Spirit. There remain elements in Hegel's view that could be thought mystical, and hence 'sacred', and he himself did not intend that the religious dimension should be eliminated; it was, rather, to be rationalized by philosophy. But even if we suppose that Hegel retains some of the essential characteristics of sacred history properly so called, during the course of the nineteenth century subsequent, successor histories of the same 'grand' sort emerged which had no place for religious meaning or the divine. The most famous of these is to be found in the writings of Karl Marx (1818–83). Set out in brief in the *Communist Manifesto* (1848) co-authored with Friedrich Engels (1820–95), and elaborated at much greater length in the unfinished three-volume work *Capital* (Volume 1, 1867). Marx's theory of history self-consciously abandons religious aspirations as products of false-consciousness and seeks their replacement with purely material (largely economic) alternatives. Marx does not invoke divine intentions but rather historical laws governing economic change—from feudal to capitalist to socialist—and the communistic classless society to which he looks as the future ideal is not a world constituted and governed by universal acknowledgement of divine rule, but one waiting to be created by imaginative human endeavour freed from the constraints of economic necessity.

Marx is not alone with his secular alternative to sacred history. Better known in their own day were the historical theories of the Frenchman Auguste Comte and the Englishman Herbert Spencer. For Comte (1798–1857), regarded by some as the founder of modern sociology, the categories of religious thought which traditional sacred histories employed, represented a primitive 'theological' stage of mind, which the philosophical rationalism of the seventeenth and eighteenth centuries had replaced and hence rendered redundant. Moreover, according to Comte, this rationalism, which he referred to as the 'metaphysical' stage of human history, was in its turn being replaced by the scientific advances of the 'positivist' period in which he himself wrote. Spencer (1820–1903), to whom we owe the expression 'survival of the fittest', also saw contemporary science as containing the means of remedying the inadequacies of religious understanding, and set about deploying, as he saw them, the insights of evolutionary theory for the purposes of constructing a new world history.

The accounts of the past elaborated by Comte or Spencer, it is true, have attracted little serious attention in this century, but no less than Marx's contention that "all history is the history of class struggle" they illustrate an important possibility, namely that attempts can be made to formulate a grand narrative of human history without the assistance, or restrictions, of revealed religion and that these attempts preserve a certain continuity with those which they sought to replace. Between the older sacred histories and their newer secular rivals there are of course marked differences. Yet there remains in them the same aspiration of looking behind the surface appearances of history, and the same belief that we need not rest content with merely recounting sequences of events in chronological order, but may properly seek to discern a meaningful direction within them.

For the sake of a label I have referred to alternatives to sacred history, such as those of Marx and Comte, as secular grand narratives. In the nineteenth century, the idea that the history of humankind in general, and the history of Western Europe in particular, displays all the marks of a progressive development struck countless thinkers and commentators as a truism and arguably Hegel, Marx and Comte are to be understood primarily as striving to give sophisticated expression to the ideas characteristic of their own age. However, the belief in progress itself is not a peculiarly nineteenth-century idea. Most recently it has been revived with considerable plausibility and sophistication by Francis Fukuyama in a widely discussed book, *The End of History and the Last Man* (1992), a work which, interestingly, he regards as something of a revival of Hegelianism, and one which will be discussed at greater length in a later chapter. Secular grand narratives need not, however, have the theoretical complexity we find in these writers. The belief in progress has, in fact, been most influential in much simpler versions. But even in these it retains the essential elements of 'grand narrative' since it seeks to discern a direction in history and attribute an overall pattern and meaning to it. Nor is this simple belief in progress, so striking in the nineteenth century, the only possible or familiar 'grand narrative' which has commanded widespread consent and shaped cultural thinking. In every age, it seems, an alternative suggestion, that history is a story of decline, has readily found adherents, especially among older generations. Moreover, the belief in historical decline, no less than the belief in progress, has generally attracted and been elaborated by those who are not content merely to chart the sequence of historical events, but to discern their general shape.

Progress and decline, then, are two familiar shapes that have often been given to the past. A third, recurrently fashionable since ancient times and one which regularly finds sophisticated exponents, is that history has moved in cycles, or perhaps more accurately, parabolas. On this view civilizations and cultures rise and fall, empires come and go and contain within themselves the elements both of their success and ultimate failure. Again, we may detect both popular and more theoretical versions of the cyclical grand narratives. The rudiments of modern more theoretical versions, such as Spengler's *Decline of the West* (1918–22), with which this chapter began, can be found in the Italian philosopher and cultural theorist Giambattista Vico (1668–1744), whose work *The New Science* (first edition 1725), though primarily concerned with larger, traditional philosophical questions, was highly innovative in this respect. A still further conception of the shape of the past takes a more schematic version, dividing history into eras. Sometimes these have been elaborate, as was the division into 'six ages' which some Christian thinkers employed, but sometimes no more complex than the common division between ancient, mediaeval, and modern periods, or the currently fashionable contrast between 'modernity' and 'postmodernism'.

More examples, and writers (Herder, Condorcet, Nietzsche, Tolstoy) could be cited but these various and familiar conceptions illustrate the nature of 'sacred' or 'metaphysical' as opposed to 'scientific' history. They all contend that despite the miasma of historical chance and change, the past has a shape. The business of discerning this shape has attracted various labels. Sacred history is one; grand narrative, world history, speculative philosophy of history and universal history are others. I shall use the term 'philosophical history' and the aim of this book is to investigate its validity. The interest in this investigation is twofold. First, there is an almost universal assumption amongst professional historians and philosophers that philosophical history is an invalid enterprise and there is a special attraction in questioning orthodox opinion. Second, notwithstanding this assumption, it is in practice hard to avoid employing some of the ideas upon which philosophical history relies. The human mind naturally seeks order and meaning, and does not easily rest content with the belief that history is, as the philosopher Bernard Bosanquet once put it, 'just one damn thing after another'. This natural tendency is frequently sustained and furthered by the ease and plausibility with which very general interpretations have been and are still imposed upon the past. Could such a recurrent endeavour on the part of so many prominent writers and thinkers be wholly misconceived?

An investigation into the validity of philosophical history as proposed here is not, however, an attempt to formulate a new grand narrative. What any such narrative requires, if it is ever to be substantiated, is an encyclopaedic body of historical fact and an adequate principle, or principles, of historical explanation. Satisfying either requirement represents an enormous undertaking, far beyond the scope of one short book. But before such a narrative could even be begun, critical and constructive thought has to be given to the conceptual structure of philosophical history in general, and to the special conceptions required by the particular varieties of narrative that different cultural theorists have espoused. In the next chapter I shall be concerned with the first of these issues, and with defending philosophical history against certain objections which, though widely accepted, have in my view won greater credibility than they warrant. In the remaining chapters I shall examine five possible kinds of philosophical history—progressivism, decline, collapse, cultural cycles, and the typological narratives of sacred history in its narrower religious sense. The examination of each of these will show, I think, that considerable philosophical sophistication is required in analysing and understanding the structure of ideas that philosophical history employs, and furthermore that sufficiently many positive conclusions can be made to emerge to make even a relatively short inquiry useful in assessing the merits of alternative conceptions. In particular, I shall argue that the originating conception of sacred history, the perception of providential purpose, has more strengths that is now generally accepted.

The full import of these remarks must await the relevant chapters, but before that it is necessary to consider briefly a very ancient, perennial and important philosophical problem which such a project may be thought to encounter. This is the dispute between Realism and Idealism in metaphysics. Broadly speaking metaphysical Realists hold that the objects of belief and knowledge are mind transcendent. That is to say, when we formulate beliefs and theories about the world we are talking about things which have a nature and existence independent of our conception of them, and science or learning is an attempt to fashion our beliefs in accordance with an external reality. Metaphysical Realism is, probably, the view that most people naturally incline to, but there is a long-standing philosophical tradition which believes it to be mistaken. This is metaphysical Idealism, which holds that it is impossible to escape the confines of ideas and language in the way that Realism requires. The human mind, according to Idealists, has immediate access only to its own contents, from which valid inferences can be drawn, certainly. But the conclusions we base upon these inferences do not allow us to reach beyond our ideas of things. They do not get us to knowledge of 'things in themselves'. The dispute between Realism and Idealism is metaphysical, about the nature of things, but also epistemological, about our knowledge of things, and this epistemological dispute may be marked by saying that, while for the Realist knowledge consists in correspondence between our ideas and the reality to which they refer, for the Idealist knowledge consists in the coherent organization of ideas and conceptions.

Realism and Idealism, thus briefly described, are not always *global* philosophical positions. That is to say, it is possible to hold a Realist view of some aspects of human thought, and an Idealist view of others. It is common, for instance, for people to take a

Realist view of natural science while taking an Idealist view of morality, holding that scientific theories relate to an external reality, but moral beliefs do not. Now it might be thought that the dispute between Realism and Idealism is crucial to philosophical history of the sort to be investigated here, because it seems important to ask whether the 'hidden' significance philosophical historians find in the events of the past is a real feature of them, or the projection on to them of the philosophical and religious ideas of the 'interpreter' of past events. If the latter, it might further be thought, we have identified an important difference between philosophical history on the one hand and scientific history on the other. It is a thought which is strengthened by the fact that Kant and Hegel, the greatest exponents of philosophical history proper, were philosophical Idealists.

But, despite this thought, and even though the disagreements between Idealism and Realism are of the greatest philosophical importance, they are not crucial to the validity of philosophical, as opposed to scientific, history. This is because Idealism and Realism are alternative accounts of human knowledge and understanding, at any and every level. Thus, since the most 'scientific' historian has to offer narratives, interpretations and explanations of the past, about all of these, no less than about the more ambitious claims of philosophical history, Idealist vs. Realist questions may be raised. Indeed 'the reality of the past' is a familiar topic amongst philosophers who concern themselves with scientific history. Conversely, a Realist who was persuaded of the merits and validity of philosophical history, would attribute a 'real' existence to the hidden meanings it uncovered.

The dispute between Idealism and Realism is thus not of *special* importance to philosophical history. It is certainly the case that, *if* it could be shown that the truth lies with metaphysical Realism, *and* that philosophical history cannot meet the requirements of a Realist conception of knowledge, this would indeed undermine the special claims, and hence distinctive enterprise of philosophical history. In this sense the debate can be said to be of great importance in this context. But given the deep-seated nature of the dispute between Realism and Idealism, any attempt to show this is unlikely to meet with success, and this has an important implication. To concentrate on this one issue because it is logically crucial, will in fact take us away from the philosophical problems unique to philosophical history.

It is more fruitful, therefore, to side-step the Realism/Idealism debate and pursue lines of inquiry directly connected with philosophical history as an enterprise. The problems encountered in doing so will form the subject-matter of the rest of this book, but something may be said here in illustration of the nature of the discussion ahead. Consider, again, the belief in progress. This might be supposed to involve nothing more than a description of the course of the past. Yet any progressivist theory of history needs not only to be able to describe the past at various stages, as scientific history attempts to do, but to relate these stages to some normative principles, such that the two, taken together, will display not merely change, but development. Moreover, a philosophical history of progress needs to demonstrate the relevance and applicability of the normative principles by which development is to be judged at, and to, all the stages it describes. Otherwise, it runs the risk of historical selectivity, of presupposing that later is better just because it is later. This necessity further requires progressivism to have a principle which explains its transhistorical applicability. Here different possibilities open up, whose relative merits have to be assessed. The higher order principle required could, for example, take the form of a relatively static theory of human nature, such as we find in Aristotle, and (I shall argue) in Francis Fukuyama, or a dialectical principle, of the sort to be found in Hegel, by which a later stage may be said to preserve and at the same time transcend the normative principles of those which preceded it. Which of these is the more plausible is a further matter to be inquired into, but the salient point to be made here is that even these brief remarks about the belief in progress, which in any case is only one possible shape we might attribute to the past, show that 'grand narrative' requires conceptual imagination and critical philosophical analysis, as well as, and no less than, historical substantiation. Without the second—historical substantiation—no finally adequate narrative can be developed. But philosophical construction is just as important and it is with this philosophical dimension that I shall be exclusively concerned.

The belief in progress construed as a philosophical history thus provides substantial material for conceptual elaboration and examination. Something of the same sort (with the relevant amendments), can be said of theories of decline. Cyclical theories, too, as we shall see, provide scope for philosophical analysis as well as historical investigation. They need, for instance, principles of identity by which the continuity and discontinuity of cultures or civilizations can be ascertained, before the course of their history can be said to display development, fulfilment and exhaustion. This preliminary philosophical analysis, I shall argue, in turn warrants a degree and level of critical attention that such theories rarely receive.

This investigation into conceptual structures, without which philosophical history cannot proceed, is one which analytical philosophy in the Anglo-Saxon tradition is admirably suited to undertake, chiefly because of the stress it has traditionally placed upon clarificatory analysis and argumentative rigour. Other philosophical traditions, broadly described as 'continental', which are generally more sympathetic to the ambitions of philosophical history, have, perhaps because of this very sympathy, tended to underplay the real difficulties which philosophical history encounters. As a result continental philosophy has usually failed to examine closely, or even display, the philosophically complex concepts which the endeavour both requires and allows. By contrast, it is the close examination of conceptual complexity in which analytical philosophy has excelled. Moreover, it need not restrict itself to mere negative criticism. There is plenty of scope within the analytical tradition for constructive analysis and conceptual imagination which will make clarity and rigour as much the allies as the enemies of philosophical history in the grand style.

That analytical philosophy in the Anglo Saxon tradition should thus be able to contribute to grand historical narratives is a contention contrary to the rather 'dry' image which it has, often justifiably, attracted to itself, and which has led some students of philosophy to turn to other traditions in the hope of more fertile, and more stimulating, intellectual ground. The primary aim of this book, however, is to reveal this as a false dichotomy, to show that a premium can be set on conceptual clarity and argumentative rigour while at the same time avoiding the theoretical or speculative aridity with which they have so often been allied. 'Does the past have a shape?' is a question which cannot but invoke the 'grand' themes of Augustine, Vico, Hegel, Marx, and Nietzsche, but answers to them which can command serious intellectual attention must have learnt from the methods of Socrates, Descartes, Wittgenstein, and Popper.

The combination of the two is still somewhat rare. Continental philosophers could be more welcoming of analytical techniques than generally they are, but more striking is the degree to which analytical philosophy has been antipathetic to the aspirations of philosophical history, and notably against the aspirations of Hegel. For this reason the next chapter must concern itself with fundamental objections to the logical possibility of philosophical history.

2 The Possibility of Philosophical History

PHILOSOPHICAL history, as its name implies, is a combination of two disciplines which are often thought to be distinct and this seems to give an initial plausibility to the sceptical belief that philosophical history has the makings of an unfortunate hybrid. However, set against this is the fact that the attempt to link philosophy with history in a single intellectual compass can be found in the writings of some of philosophy's most respected practitioners. Indeed, it is to Immanuel Kant (1724–1804), undoubtedly one of the greatest of all metaphysicians and moral philosophers, that we owe explicit formulation of *The Idea of a Universal History from a Cosmopolitan Point of View*, the long title of a short essay, published in 1784. In this essay Kant maintains that though the empirical study of historical phenomena is essential to understanding the human past, in itself it is insufficient, since the plans of individuals, however rational, taken on their own cannot explain the emergence of developing forms of thought and civil association. The most individuals can do, either singly or collectively in societies, is to act within the limited circumstances and short historical perspective in which they find themselves. Yet there are, Kant contends, general trends to be observed in the history of humankind. We cannot sensibly attribute these to the purposes of individuals, even in concert, but being none the less observed historical phenomena, they demand explanation if we are to have any serious intellectual concern with the past. Their explanation, Kant believed, must impute to the historical process a natural teleology, a purpose or end which Nature or Providence (he uses both terms) develops through the rational agency of human beings.

Kant's essay, to the themes of which we will have occasion to return, is merely an outline of a possible form of inquiry, and in it he looks to the emergence of an equivalent in this sphere of a Kepler or a Newton in physical science, someone intellectually equipped to compose a genuinely universal history which will reveal the underlying rationale of the past in the way that Kepler and Newton uncovered the underlying rationality of the physical universe. Such a figure as Kant anticipates might have been thought to be found in his celebrated successor, Hegel, whose *Lectures on the Philosophy of World History* probably constitute the most sustained effort ever made in this aspect of philosophy. However, Hegelian philosophy of history, and with it the whole endeavour to produce a universal history, is now largely out of fashion, especially in the circles of traditional analytical philosophy, and has been so for some considerable time. The reason for this has much to do with the general dominance of positivistic conceptions of knowledge for most of this century, and in particular Karl Popper's application of the falsifiability criterion of science to Hegelian philosophy in the second volume of his famous book *The Open Society and its Enemies*, which develops a similar line of thought to that found in earlier British critics of Hegel, notably L. T. Hobhouse and Bertrand Russell. By Popper's account scientific knowledge (by which we should understand him to mean *real* knowledge), is marked by its susceptibility to falsification, and Hegel's philosophy of history, like its less philosophical successor, Marxism, is vitiated by its manipulation of evidence to avoid falsification. Rather than the theory being answerable to the facts scientific history uncovers, the 'facts' are made to answer to the theory. Hegel and Marx do not tell us how the past *was*, but how, in the light of their theories, it *must have been*. In this way, though they masquerade as historians, they in fact pass beyond the realms of empirical history, and the theses advanced, though they may superficially look like historical theories, are in fact unfalsifiable a-priori assertions.

So, at any rate, this line of thought made familiar by Popper contends. Popper (like Hobhouse) also believed that Hegel's approach to philosophy, which he labelled 'historicism', gave philosophical succour to totalitarian regimes, and this association with an unpalatable political ideology further contributed to the rejection of Hegel. In fact, Popper's charges in this respect are unfounded. As *The Cambridge Companion to Hegel* puts it— "If we carefully examine all the passages from Hegel's writings in which he draws some political point from history, we find that . . . Hegel appealed to history to justify the middle path of reform, to criticize both radicals and reactionaries alike . . . In the spectrum of political belief in Germany after the French Revolution, Hegel reveals himself to be a progressive moderate" (Beiser, pp. 293–4). Hegel's political philosophy is best understood, in fact, as an alternative explanation of the basis and value of individual freedom, not a defence of its restriction. Accordingly it is the methodological objection which is the more important. But there must be added to it the serious doubts most practising historians have had about the inevitable overgeneralization involved in *any* attempt to consider the whole sweep of history. Together these objections provide a ready explanation of the unpopularity of philosophical history. They imply that neither philosophy nor history can confirm, or even accommodate, the Hegelian enterprise. In short, from at least two points of view philosophical history seems intrinsically *doomed* to failure, and this degree of pessimism about its possibility is widely thought to have been vindicated by the demonstrably unsuccessful attempts of those, like Oswald Spengler and Arnold Toynbee, who have engaged in it.

Yet, whatever the general consensus of philosophers and historians may be, many of the elements of philosophical history continue to play an important, though largely unrecognized part in the most fashionable philosophical theories, and this gives us good reason to reconsider the basis of its rejection. For instance, the popular concern with postmodernism cannot but invoke a grand historical classification—the period of modernity and its aftermath, since it is quite implausible to understand by 'modernity' and 'postmodernity' simple cultural or political events; they are, rather, eras or epochs which are to be identified and characterized by the ideas which dominated them, and this is precisely the sort of conception which the vilified philosophical theorist of history typically employs. 'Modernity' is not a period identified simply in terms of dates, but a cultural era, with its own intellectual and political 'project'. Discussion of the importance of modernity and postmodernism, consequently, is one way in which philosophical history comes into play in contemporary philosophy, even if this is not always recognized. More important perhaps (since the idea of 'postmodernism' does not command respect from philosophers in every quarter), is the widespread revival of interest in Hegel. While it seems that there are few enthusiastic supporters for Hegel's philosophy of history in contemporary Western philosophy, there are many who believe that the wholesale rejection of Hegel by analytic philosophers in the first half of this century was a serious error. Yet, to return to Hegel without returning to philosophical history implies a selective rejection and acceptance of his philosophy which is not easy to defend. This is because Hegel's philosophy is historical through and through. As Frederick Beiser writes: "History cannot be consigned to a corner in Hegel's system, relegated to a few paragraphs near the end of the *Encyclopaedia* or confined to his *Lecture on the Philosophy of History* . . . history is central to Hegel's conception of philosophy" (Beiser, p. 270).

This conception holds that all genuine knowledge and understanding is the outcome of an historical process which has its special, discoverable rationale and culmination; to grasp them is the task of philosophy. In elaborating this contention Hegel could indeed be guilty of historical apriorism and overgeneralization. Those, including Popper, who have brought this objection do not always seem aware that both accusations are potential criticisms which Hegel himself acknowledged, and which in several places he strives to answer, as does Kant before him. Both Kant and Hegel recognize that philosophical history must acknowledge the need for empirical inquiry into the contingent course of events. But equally they argue for the necessity of conceptual, and hence philosophical, inquiry in any adequate understanding of the past. In making this second claim they could indeed be mistaken, but since they make strenuous efforts to address the problem, it cannot be sufficient ground for condemning their enterprise merely to observe that the problem exists. A certain kind of crude apriorism in history, which speaks much too readily of the inevitable in advance of establishing the facts—historicism—is possible. It is also obviously objectionable. What is much less clear is that the deficiencies of this crude version will inevitably be found in any and every elaboration of Kant's or Hegel's contention about philosophy and the past.

There is, then, reason to reserve judgement on their enterprise, and we may strengthen our reservation by adding this further observation: at the heart of the positivist/Popperian objection to Hegelian philosophical history is the belief that we must not confuse, or compound, the empirical and the logical, the historical and the conceptual. According to this objection, while the empirical and historical concern themselves with what, contingently, *is* the case, the logical and conceptual are concerned with the realm of necessity, what *must* be so. The two are logically distinct and there is thus no place for the hybrid 'historical necessity', which is the idea upon which Hegelian philosophy of history is thought by its critics to rely so heavily. Interestingly, however, this strict division between the logical and the empirical itself relies upon a thesis which has come under attack in analytical philosophy. This is the thesis which the twentieth-century American philosopher W. V. Quine famously declared a *dogma* of empiricism, namely the belief that there is a radical distinction between conceptual questions and matters of brute fact. It is a dogma, Quine thinks, because it is a presupposition, not a conclusion, of empiricist philosophy. This is classically the case with David Hume, whose *Treatise of Human Nature* starts out with an assertion of the distinction between 'relations of ideas' and 'matters of real existence' and proceeds to demolish many familiar lines of thought on the basis of it. The power of the arguments seems to support his empiricist distinction, but if we were to deny the appropriateness of his starting place, many of the arguments would come to nothing.

It is striking that Quine's rejection of this distinction should have found widespread support. Moreover it has prompted much greater sympathy than was formerly the case with those broadly 'anti-analytical' currents in continental philosophy which have stressed the importance of the historical and social context of philosophical inquiry. As a result, a large amount of attention has recently been given not only to Hegel, but to Nietzsche, Michel Foucault, Hans-Georg Gadamer and a wide range of other continental philosophers by those brought up in the Anglo-Saxon tradition. But if, in line with this strand of thinking, a strict separation between the logical and the empirical is indeed to be regarded as a dogma of empiricism, and an indefensible one, what then was Hegel's fault? One suggestion is this. Hegel is not wrong to think in terms that deny a logical gap between the conceptual and the factual; his mistake was to try to bridge it in the wrong way. He brings philosophy to bear on history, rather than bringing history to bear upon philosophy. Philosophical concepts have a history; that is why philosophy cannot ignore their historical development. But Hegel speaks as though history can be construed as a philosophical development. To abandon Hegelian philosophy of history, therefore, is not to suppose that there is after all a radical gulf between history and philosophy, but only that Hegel tries to cross it from the wrong direction.

There is a sizeable body of opinion, I think, which would regard this response as plausible. In this chapter I shall argue to the contrary that it is inadequate. My contention will be first, that an argument can be made to show that for certain, respectable purposes, the bringing of philosophy to bear upon history is unavoidable, and in so far as philosophy is properly thought of as an a priori inquiry, Kant and Hegel are therefore correct in thinking that historical understanding must concern itself with the a priori as well as the a posteriori, with the conceptually adequate as well as the historically accurate. I shall further argue that some prominent concerns in contemporary Anglo-Saxon philosophy are in fact elaborations of a philosophical history, and that they implicitly attribute a shape to the past. This will set the stage for subsequent chapters in which various 'shapes', including that which is to be found in Kant and Hegel, are more explicitly examined.

I

It is best to begin the argument, however, at some considerable remove from the rather lofty concerns of universal history by considering a very simple example in which an episode in the past is related. Suppose I wish to tell you about a special dinner that turned into a fiasco. I must of course purport to tell you what happened, and in so doing can deviate from or adhere to truth and accuracy. The practice of embellishing stories is thoroughly familiar, and in some cases people who embellish may genuinely misremember in their desire to make their story more interesting, significant, or amusing. Let us agree that history 'proper', even in this homely sort of case, must renounce gratuitous embellishment and acknowledge the necessity of strict adherence to truth. Even so, there is more to telling the story successfully than the simple recipe 'tell us what happened' might be taken to imply. We need a grasp on relevance as well as truth.

The point may be made by reference to the 'Ideal Chronicler', a familiar device in philosophy of history, and one which has been widely used to test and explore various conceptions of historical inquiry. 'Ideal Chronicler' is the name given to some recording machine or other means of observation of the present which, by hypothesis, omits nothing that happens, and so, as time passes, gives us a complete record of the past, a record which contains every single event. Equally familiar to philosophers of history is an argument to the effect that the idea of such a device is internally incoherent. According to this argument events are not singly countable in the way that the concept of an ideal chronicle requires—is a battle one event or innumerably many?—and the identification of events requires active interpretation which the passivity of the imaginary device does not possess. Hence it makes no sense to speak of automatically recording all the events of a given period.

These are both good objections, in my view, but even if we were to reject them and accept that the Ideal Chronicler is a coherent conception, it is nevertheless apparent that no such device at our dinner party could, without amendment, provide us with the story we are seeking. This is for the rather obvious reason that a great many events which happened in the course of the evening are not *relevant* to that story; though they did indeed happen, they reveal nothing about how the dinner turned into a fiasco. Some such events will not figure in the story because they are inherently trivial—a knife or fork becoming dirty as it is used, a wineglass becoming wet as wine is poured into it for instance. Other happenings, on the face of it trivial—nose blowings, for example, or many of the remarks made at table—could in principle have been significant; a chance remark made in a sudden silence can take on unintended significance. But as it turns out, none of these play a part in this particular story. Yet other events, say for instance the making of new business contacts, which may be highly significant in other stories, need have no bearing on this story—how the dinner turned into a fiasco. Indeed, there is every reason to suppose that even if there were an Ideal Chronicle of the dinner, that is, a complete record of all that happened between the beginning and the end, the vast majority of events it recorded would in all likelihood be irrelevant to what concerns us—the telling of *this* story.

In addition to concern with truth, then, even simple history requires a concern with relevance. Such a conclusion is neither novel nor startling, but it is none the less of some importance and is a point to which we will have to return. However, before doing so we should make the further observation that truth and relevance are not all that must come into play. A sense of the *purpose* of the story-telling is also required. In this example, the purpose is perhaps amusement (though other, larger purposes can readily be imagined). Two things are worth noticing about this further condition. First, amusement cannot be taken to mean whatever happens to amuse. A story that starts out to be amusing, may amuse and yet also take on something of the malicious. Context and intention are important as well as effect. Second, not all purposes are mutually exclusive. This is of special significance once we go beyond homely examples and into the realms of, say, academic history. It is commonly supposed that the purpose of history proper is to inform rather than, say, to entertain. But this is a false dichotomy. It is clear in the example I have been exploring that the listener will be amused *by being* informed, at least if truth and accuracy continue to be observed. So too with history proper. The provision of accurate historical information is one purpose historical narrative may serve. But it can serve larger purposes also, without, importantly, thereby ceasing to be the provision of information. The truth of this opens up a further significant possibility, that history in its most sophisticated forms, even if it may never cease to make the provision of reliable information one of its main concerns, may also serve and be expected to serve purposes which go beyond that.

The lesson to be drawn from this example and these remarks is this. Concern with truth and accuracy is insufficient for the recounting of historical episodes. We also need a clear grasp of the relevance of the material to be employed and a conception of the point of employing it. Without these further elements, the business of history cannot really begin. However, once attention has been drawn to considerations of relevance and purpose as well as truth and accuracy, we have also admitted a space in the structure of narrative within which, interestingly, philosophy can be brought to bear upon history, though it is important to stress that this is only a possibility. It is only in some cases that the bringing of philosophy to bear upon historical narrative is either necessary or desirable.

To demonstrate both these points it is helpful to look at another simple example. Suppose I am recounting the course of an election. Granted that what has been said so far is correct, my narrative, in addition to a faithful account of the unfolding of events, must have some determinate purpose which it is intended to serve and must employ some criterion of relevance. In this example, as in many others, the first plays a large part in establishing the second; what is relevant is determined chiefly by the point of the story. Let us imagine that the point of the history of the election is to explain why the winners won. If so, between the time at which the election was called and that at which the winners were declared, there will have been a great many events, including events properly described as political, which are irrelevant to the explanatory account. What makes these irrelevant? We might begin an answer to this question by saying that irrelevant events are those which had no bearing on the outcome of the election, and by 'outcome' we will mean, largely, the number of votes cast for each party. This is only the beginning of an answer because 'having a bearing upon' is not a very precise phrase. But it will do to illustrate an important point. The *terminus ad quem*, the end point of the narrative, is in this case an electoral victory, and though there may be disputes about whether the outcome was properly arrived at—disputes that is to say about the legitimacy of the procedure—given that it was legitimate, what *counts* as an electoral victory is not open to much dispute (in reasonably stable constitutional conditions). Victory goes to those with the greatest number of votes.

But it is not hard to imagine examples in which the *terminus ad quem* of an historical explanation is conceptually more uncertain. Suppose that, rather than seeking to explain simple electoral victory—the numerical outcome of voting—we seek to explain the triumph of democracy over demagoguery or dictatorship. In this case we are faced not merely with the task of explaining why what happened happened, but with assessing whether the events we recount add up to something called a 'triumph for democracy'. Rather evidently, this requires some reflection on the concept of democracy, since in contrast to simple electoral victory, there is a good deal to be said about what counts as 'democracy'.

Of course, professional historians may, and do, eschew such reflection, especially if it is couched in such relatively flowery phrases as 'triumph of democracy'. They might claim, as many have, that scientific history or history proper ought not to include value judgements of this kind. The desire to exclude value judgements from history is not ultimately defensible, in my view, but the point here is rather this; that high level historical narratives cannot avoid the use of sophisticated concepts like 'democracy'. It is a poor conception of history that does not permit it to recount, for example, the emergence of modern science or the development of political liberalism, both of which are strikingly important features of the recent past and of contemporary culture.

The writing of either of these histories will require not merely a concern with truth and relevance, but a clear understanding of the concepts of science and liberalism.

The point and purpose of an historical narrative, then, its *terminus ad quem*, will often employ abstract concepts of the sort with which philosophy typically deals. By itself this does not show that philosophy has a bearing upon history. A further question may yet be raised, as to whether this employment and the clear conceptual understanding it requires jointly or severally imply the need for philosophical *inquiry*. It has frequently been noted, in a variety of philosophical contexts, that to understand a concept, even a complex concept, we do not need to be able to *articulate* that understanding. The ability to *understand* the grammar of a language, which all language users have, does not imply (or require) an ability to *formulate* it. Explicit formulation of grammatical rules is a skill independent of that required to speak a language. In a similar fashion, even if it is true, as I have been arguing, that composing historical narratives at the highest levels requires a prior understanding of such sophisticated concepts as 'science' and 'liberalism', it does not follow that the historian has to engage in the philosophical explication or refinement of those concepts. It is sufficient for historians to have a tacit understanding of the concepts they employ. It is not necessary that they be able to make that understanding philosophically explicit. In other words, to agree that philosophy is concerned with conceptual questions and at the same time to accept that history requires conceptual understanding does not carry the implication that philosophy has, or even can have, a bearing on history.

II

This seems correct. There is indeed a hiatus in the argument. The move from philosophy's concern with concepts and history's presupposition of concepts to the legitimacy of philosophical history in the Hegelian style, though it has sometimes been made, is facile. These two facts in combination do not in themselves show that philosophical inquiry has a bearing upon the writing of history in any substantial sense. But neither do they rule it out. What is needed here is an argument to show first, that at least on occasions, historical writing will be defective without some conceptual refinement and further, that philosophical method is the most appropriate means by which such refinement is to be attained.

The possibility of an argument arises where the concepts the historian is required to employ are contested, which is to say open to dispute. It was the historian and philosopher W. B. Gallie, in a once famous essay, who introduced the idea of essentially contested concepts. By calling them *essentially* contested he meant to draw attention to what he regarded as an intrinsic feature of them, namely that what such concepts denote and connote is not just contingently a matter of disagreement, but inherently so. Examples of the sort of concept he had in mind are not far to seek. What we are to *count* as socialism, or democracy, or Christianity, or science, are all matters upon which disagreement has been generated and about which a range of recognizable positions has emerged. Some of these examples are Gallie's, in fact, and they will usefully serve present purposes. But two important qualifications need to be entered. The first is that we do not have to agree with the more ambitious claim of *essential* contestability in order to agree that, as a matter of fact, these, amongst others, are real instances of contested concepts. That is to say, we can accept that there are deep disagreements between recognizable positions about these specific concepts, while remaining agnostic about whether this fact is to be explained by their logical structure or by historical genesis. We can accept, for example, that there are legitimate disputes about whether Mormonism is to count as a variety of Christianity, without agreeing that the origin of this dispute lies in the fact that the content of Christianity is by its very nature contestable. The second qualification is this;

all the examples listed above invoke normative or evaluative elements, though this is not always made plain by the listing of such concepts alone. In fact, what is really contested is better described as the content of *true* socialism, democracy *proper*, *orthodox* Christianity, or *real* science. This normative dimension is interesting and important in a number of respects, but making it explicit here alerts us to a danger which, arguably, is realized in Gallie's own essay. This is the danger of conflating a claim about the logic of certain specific concepts with the quite general application of a familiar thesis about the irresolvability of normative disputes. Many people think that all questions of value, by their very nature, do not admit of one rationally defensible answer. But this is a *different* claim to the claim that certain concepts, such as Christianity or socialism, are essentially contestable.

For present purposes, it is of considerable importance not to get entangled in this general issue about values. Let us suppose it is true quite generally that at some level normative disputes are not rationally resolvable. Even so, it may still be possible to distinguish different levels of dispute, and not all of these are necessarily irresolvable. It may therefore be the case that the sorts of dispute between competing conceptions with which we are here concerned arise at these lower, resolvable, levels. To take a trivial example, it could be that a preference for red wine over white cannot be given a rational basis, but that preferences between reds can. A more significant example might be this: though there have for a long time been deep-seated disagreements about the justification of punishment, it may nevertheless be possible to produce rational agreement that some specific punishment is unjust. Legal theorists dispute whether the best explanation is to be found in deterrence, retribution or reform, but even if it is not possible to arrive at a single universally accepted conception of the justification of punishment, protagonists of all camps might concur in the belief that ten years imprisonment for a parking offence is unjust.

These examples are consistent with the assumption that

normative disagreements are ultimately irresolvable. If, alternatively, we assume that normative disputes *are* ultimately resolvable, it may still be the case that some kinds of conceptual conflict inherently are not. 'Audible' I take it, is not a normative concept, but it is plausible to hold that it makes no sense to try to decide whether a sound that can be heard by bats but not by human beings is to be regarded as audible *per se* or not. The conclusion to be drawn is that either way, whether matters of value are or are not ultimately determinable, the nature of disputes involving competing conceptions can be regarded as a question independent of the nature of normativity in general.

Pace Gallie, then, we need not assume that it is the normative nature of many competing conceptions which makes them *essentially* contested. Nor are we obliged to assume that where conceptions are as a matter of fact contested, there is no available rational procedure for adjudicating between them. The only point at issue here is whether the telling of an historical story sometimes requires an articulate examination of competing conceptions and not merely an implicit understanding of concepts. This is a matter which can, I have been arguing, be held apart from more abstract disputes about the nature of normative judgement in general.

However, some of the examples given—Christianity, socialism and democracy, for instance—make the holding apart of these two issues rather hard to achieve. This is because they are all conceptions commonly associated with and surrounded by complex arguments and long-standing allegiances. The nature of contested concepts and their role in historical narrative may be more easily illustrated, therefore, by the fourth example, that of scientific advance.

What is to count as an advance in science? This is a question that it is impossible for the history of science to avoid. Take, for example, the history of psychiatry. It is plain enough that there is such a history to be recounted. We can trace the beginnings of human understanding of the workings of the mind, and chart phases in its development. It is implausible to think that all stages or phases in this development have been of equal influence and importance. Psychologists and psychiatrists have made many important discoveries, but like all other scientists they have also entered blind alleys. One question which the history of psychiatry must contend with is the place of Sigmund Freud and psychoanalysis in the narrative. No one could seriously deny that Freudianism should figure in some way or other in this history, given the prominence and influence it has enjoyed in the twentieth century. It is a matter of contention, however, whether it should figure as a major advance, one not yet fully capitalized upon, or as a misbegotten adventure into which the subject was led to its detriment.

Now this issue cannot be resolved, or even addressed, without some explicit examination of the intellectual merits of psychoanalysis as science. The important point to notice for present purposes is this: the need to enter the debate about the scientific status of psychoanalysis arises from an eminently respectable historical purpose, that of trying to construct an adequate history of psychiatry. 'Science' is a label to which status and prestige attaches, and rightly so, but one consequence of this is that arguments over what is and is not science tend to arouse partisan feeling and deep division. This has proved specially marked in the particular case of psychoanalysis. Indeed, at one period so much academic axe-grinding surrounded the issue, that the scientific status of Freudian theory, and psychoanalysis in general, became highly contested in a public and very obvious sense of 'contested'. This deep contention is a fact of cultural history, and one which provides credence (though not in my view evidence) for claims about the incommensurability of conceptions of science. But the point to be emphasized here is this: it is possible to regard such disputes with disdain, and to be quite unconcerned with the practical implications that have been seen in them, and at the same time acknowledge the importance of exploring the issue that lies at their heart—the scientific status of psychoanalysis. Moreover we must do so if we are to carry out the relatively simple purpose of recounting the history of psychiatry.

Once this necessity is recognized, it is a small step to the recognition that concern with this issue cannot but raise philosophical questions about the nature of science. And as a matter of fact, where passion has abated and the status of psychoanalysis has been carefully and systematically explored, major contributions to the debate have been made by established philosophers of science.

It follows that for the historian of psychiatry, normative philosophical issues about the nature of science are part and parcel of the inquiry, and in this restricted but important sense, philosophy can, in this case if no other, be shown to have a bearing upon history. The scientific status of psychoanalysis is only one example, certainly. I do not think it is specially difficult to supply others. But even one example is sufficient to illustrate the logical possibility of philosophy's having a bearing upon history. Practising historians are almost certain to regard such a conclusion with suspicion, and some of the grounds for this suspicion do need to be explored further. Empiricist-minded historians may insist that their task is merely to record what happened in the past and not to decide whether what happened was good or bad. Indeed, they might claim, it is precisely a recognition of the need for history proper to make and abide by such a distinction that led to the abandonment of narrative in the style of the so-called Whig interpretation of history (history as a battle between the forces of enlightenment and the forces of reaction), now generally derided by professional historians, a derision nicely captured in *1066 and All That* where rulers and events are regularly classified as 'a good thing' or 'a bad thing'. In the present case there is no need, this empiricist line of thought supposes, to decide whether something is or is not science, but only to record whether it was or was not so regarded. So, the history of psychiatry does not need to decide whether psychoanalysis is truly scientific, but only to record whether, and for how long, the practitioners of psychiatry saw it as such.

Whether this empiricist objection to philosophy in history can ultimately be sustained is too large an issue to examine in detail here. But even if we were to agree that there is no *need* to proceed further than the strictly empirical in this sense, what has to be shown is that it is senseless or improper to try to do more, and a mere taste or preference for more straightforward and less contentious inquiry does not show that it is. We know that people can be mistaken, and with the benefit of hindsight even come to regard themselves as such. What may in popular consciousness pass for a time as a great victory, for instance, may subsequently prove to have been based more on illusion than on reality. The recording of such errors is, it seems to me, a perfectly respectable task for the historian to engage in, and only an unfounded fear of being improperly judgemental argues against it. Indeed, as has often been remarked by philosophers of history, it is only with a perspective on the past that is not available contemporaneously that a proper account of events can be given. This perspective is sometimes discounted as an illegitimate reliance on the benefit of hindsight, but it is hard to see how the invocation of hindsight, more respectably called 'historical perspective', could be avoided. Those events which constitute the first and last shots in the American Civil War, for example, could not have been known to be such by those who witnessed them. Only with hindsight can we know them to be what they were. Similarly with the history of science; discoveries contemporaneously regarded as insignificant may be known only later to be the breakthroughs they were. Mendel's observations in genetics provide a plausible instance. So too with psychoanalysis. From the point of view of good history we must indeed avoid the distortion which the imposition of modern assumptions upon the past may produce, but neither need we take the opinions of contemporaries of earlier periods as specially authoritative. We can have good reason to prefer the point of view which benefits from historical retrospective.

This way of putting it raises a further question. What makes this historical perspective *preferable* rather than merely *different*? What makes the point of view formed with hindsight *better* and not merely *later*? To answer this we need to look a little more closely at the source of historians' anxieties about the role of philosophy as I have described it. The conclusion of the argument so far is that on occasions philosophically grounded understanding of the concepts to be employed in a narrative may make for better history. We might sum up the historian's anxiety about this as a fear of apriorism. There is a widespread conviction that there *must* be something wrong with the suggestion that the concepts history employs can be formulated in advance and in abstraction of historical inquiry itself, because there can be no guarantee that independently formulated concepts will have any application in history at all. For example, suppose it is true that we can only decide whether Freudianism was an advance or a sidetrack in the history of psychiatry if we take some view about the nature of science. This certainly seems to require a philosophical examination of the concept of science. But an analysis of concepts *wholly* abstracted from experience, an exercise in 'pure' thought of the sort philosophy seems typically to engage in, may well produce a conception of science which, as a matter of fact, bears no relation at all to the history of psychiatry as it has been. What, the historian might ask, is to restrain the conceptual imagination with a view to relevance, if it is not the realities of the past itself?

This is an important question, and in part it explains a recurrent doubt about philosophical history in the Hegelian style, namely that being freed from the constraints of historical fact, it is licenced, or considers itself licenced, to pontificate about how the past *must* have been, rather than, in a more pedestrian, empirical fashion, being content with recording how it *was*. This doubt, and indeed the danger that it is too easily realized when philosophy is brought to bear upon history, are both legitimate concerns. It is not sufficient, however, to respond to them by retreating to a strictly descriptive, and hence impoverished, history. This too rests upon a dichotomy between the descriptive and the conceptual that is overdrawn. Those who believe, because of the arguments adduced and the examples given, that philosophy may indeed have a bearing upon history, can equally insist that history must also have a bearing upon philosophy. Such an insistence, it seems to me, is not a departure from Hegel, but an endorsement of one of his central contentions. In a celebrated phrase, Hegel contends that the owl of Minerva, which is to say philosophical wisdom, can rise only at dusk, that is, only with the benefit of historical hindsight, and this seems to give history some control over philosophical speculation. A similar thought is to be found in the approach to science taken by Thomas Kuhn in *The Structure of Scientific Revolutions*; good philosophy of science requires a good knowledge of the history of science.

III

The point we have reached is this. An argument may be constructed to show that historical narrative requires active engagement with philosophical issues of a conceptually normative kind. Such an argument proceeds by steps. Historians may, if they choose, restrict themselves to recording how events were contemporaneously perceived, but, as many would agree, a preference for doing so does not show that there is anything illegitimate about constructing a narrative which makes use of historical perspective and the benefits of hindsight. However, such a perspective will commonly employ ideas of success and failure, advance and decline, and these are concepts which frequently require philosophical analysis and conceptual imagination.

It is the introduction of such ideas, with their seemingly context-free analysis, which generates the fear that judgements about advance and decline, success and failure, become importantly ahistorical, dislocated from the facts of history, and sustained by abstract argument to a degree which permits the worst excesses of apriorism, an approach to the past in which grand 'theory' is allowed to determine fact in advance of (and hence irrespective of) serious historical investigation. To make good the claims of philosophical history to be a valid intellectual enterprise, therefore, some account of its ultimate, if not immediate, answerability to historical realities must be given.

This last demand, it seems to me, is substantially correct, and it needs to be explored further if the possibility of philosophical history is to be defended adequately. Here we will do better to leave the relatively restricted example of psychiatry, and consider instead the case of science in general. In telling the story of science, its beginnings, growth, and development, assessments of significance will have to figure prominently. What takes such a history beyond the mundane level of 'first this, then that' is a narrative of accomplishment and setback, development and regression, innovation and futility. All these concepts are normative, but, whatever the beliefs of the empirical historian, without them we simply do not have a properly narrative structure. In developing such a narrative there are at least two perspectives to be accommodated, that from which the story begins and that with which it ends, and there is also the necessity of formulating some relationship between them. This relationship is not a simple one; it cannot be construed along the lines of the relationship between the roof of a house and its foundations. Here the case of science is instructive. The early Greeks, amongst whose intellectual endeavours we may find the origins of what we now call science, could not have conceived of much, if anything, that is common to its contemporary practice. The concepts and explanatory techniques of quantum physics find no counterpart in their ancient progenitors. Conversely, contemporary science cannot find anything relevant to the advance of its current concerns in the surviving fragments of the pre-Socratics. Yet, despite this great gulf, the two are undoubtedly connected and continuous. The task of the historian is to find a story of continuity which will span this evident discontinuity, and the task of the philosopher of history is to display, and hence on occasions make available, the conceptual structure of any such story. It is in this way that conceptual necessity bears upon empirical history.

It is with the philosopher's task that we are here concerned. How should we conceive the relationship between modern science and its ancient origins? We can begin by observing the inappropriateness of two possible models. The first is what, following Alasdair MacIntyre (in *Three Rival Versions of Moral Inquiry*), we might call the 'encyclopaedic' model. The encyclopaedic model construes the history of science as the steady accumulation of knowledge of fact, and hence the development of science as essentially a quantitative expansion in which facts are added to facts. The inadequacy of this model is evident. Both the facts and the explanations in which modern science trades, couched as they are in the language of sophisticated mathematics, could not have been conceived of, still less sought for, by the pre-Socratics. Conversely, there is nothing in the pre-Socratic writings of Thales or Anaximander which would count in the modern period as knowledge of well-attested fact. It follows that the encyclopaedic model, wherever else it might apply, cannot be correct for the history of science.

An alternative model is that of the abstract essentialist. This conceives of science as a single unchanging endeavour, characterized by epistemologically validated ends which are more fully realized in later than in earlier periods of history. One such conception might be the idea that real science consists in deductively valid explanations derived from lawlike generalizations rooted in experimentally attested fact. But once again, this model will not serve the purpose of recounting the history of science either. If the essence of science so conceived makes allowance for the sophistication of modern quantum physics, it must by the same token regard most past science, which falls so far short of this ideal, as 'science so-called'. As a result, the endeavours of even major figures in its history, such as Aristotle or Copernicus, will have to be construed as colossal failures hugely wide of the mark. Such a view is faulty in two respects; it implicitly but illicitly assumes a modern perspective, and it is ahistorical. That is to say, it picks arbitrarily on just one period, the modern period, as the exemplar of 'real science', and wholly disregards the historically located tasks and ambitions of those in the past who have regarded themselves as scientists, and been regarded famously as such. Nor is this ahistoricity a consequence of a prejudice in favour of the modern. The same would be true whatever point in the past we chose to represent the essence of science proper. If Aristotelian biology is given this status, Darwinian biology, which has no place for the teleology of species, must be discounted.

Neither the encyclopaedic nor essentialist models then, will answer the purpose of providing an adequate conceptual structure for the narrative history of science. There is however a third possibility. This is one which embodies the important recognition that it is not only the *achievements* of early science that are outmoded, but the very *aims* which lent those achievements their importance. At the same time, it recognizes that there is a story to be told of phases and stages in which scientific aims were transformed and transcended in a way which both preserved something of them and altered them, eventually beyond immediate recognition. On this third conception, it is only in full recognition of these two facts that historical narrative can give a proper account of both continuity and discontinuity, revealing how origin and end can be continuous and at the same time wholly different.

This third model, as the terminology I have used to describe it suggests, invokes something similar to Hegel's notion of *Aufhebung*, which Michael Inwood translates as 'sublation' and which, he says "means (1) 'raising up'; (2) 'abolition'; and (3) 'preserving'" (*A Hegel Dictionary* p. 283). We are thus brought back to the central concerns of this chapter, the legitimacy of philosophical history. The concept of *aufheben*, which is central to Hegel's account of 'world history', is a concept widely regarded as mysterious, but we have now located it at work in a fairly clear and determinate context, and given reason for thinking that some such concept may be necessary in the writing of history. This shows, I hope, that *aufheben* can be given a relatively demystified explication. What is important to observe, however, is the way in which this central concept of Hegel's philosophy of history should dispel the historian's anxiety about apriorism. It is in fact not the third but the second model I described, the essentialist model, which is aprioristic, and indeed internally incoherent. For while essentialism is apparently removed from the vagaries of the historical process, in reality it assumes the special importance of just one point in history, in my example 'the present'. If, however, I have described the model properly called Hegelian correctly, the standards of knowledge and understanding which modern science seeks to satisfy are themselves to be explained as the outcome of an historical process which preserves a continuity with earlier standards now superseded. The standards of good science that we commonly accept are to be vindicated as good by the inquiries of normative philosophy, but they are to be vindicated as the standards of good *science* by history. In this way, if it is true, as I have been arguing, that philosophy can and sometimes must have a bearing upon history, it is also true that history has a bearing upon philosophy.

Hegel does indeed assume the superiority of the point of view of the present in the formulation of his conceptual apparatus. But he does not do so arbitrarily. In the passage from *The Philosophy of Right*, which I have already quoted, where he observes that 'the owl of Minerva takes its flight only at dusk', he means to say that philosophy itself requires the hindsight which only the end of an historical process can give. Our contemporary conception of science (my example not his) is superior, but only in the sense that it derives from the perspective from which alone an adequate narrative of development can be told. It is not that, in the style of essentialism, contemporary scientists have a peculiar grasp of the true nature of science which previous generations of so-called scientists somewhat curiously lacked. We have such a grasp precisely because of our historical position relative to them. We have come later as a matter of historical record, and the end, or at least the later stages of the story, are preferable from the point of view of understanding, just because they are later and explanations benefit from hindsight.

IV

Arriving at this conclusion accomplishes the first of the objectives of this chapter, namely defending the legitimacy of philosophical history. The defence consists in establishing the necessity of normative philosophical analysis and conceptual imagination in the construction of some historical narratives, while at the same time preserving the necessity of historical constraints upon our philosophical endeavours. Philosophy has a bearing upon history which in turn has a bearing upon philosophy. This is, in effect, a defence of the rudiments of Hegelian philosophy of history, formulated in full recognition of the need to avoid the charge of apriorism.

The chapter has two further objectives—to show that an important component of modern philosophy is an engagement in philosophical history and to show that this inevitably means its attributing a shape to the past. Both these further objectives are more rapidly established against the background of the foregoing arguments.

One relatively straightforward way of supporting the contention that contemporary philosophy has its philosophical historians is to assemble a few instances—examples, that is to say, of prominent philosophical writers whose views are only intelligible if set in the context of a philosophical history. Richard Rorty is one of these. In his celebrated book *Philosophy and the Mirror of Nature* Rorty advances the thesis that the history of Western philosophy is a story of the pursuit of the impossible. It is in fact a catalogue of failure. At the heart of the traditional Western philosophical enterprise, he argues, lies an attempt to secure knowledge against the uncertainties of contingency by removing it from the inevitably relativizing influences of human thought and perception. Both the rationalism of René Descartes (1596–1650) and the empiricism of John Locke (1632–1704) are to be understood in this way. They seek to construct an account of thought which will allow it to be a wholly neutral conduit through which, as it were, reality in itself can flow untainted, or to use Rorty's own metaphor, an inactive glass which merely mirrors nature. What this ambition ultimately requires, Rorty claims, is the idea of thought without a thinking subject, a logical impossibility. But we will only grasp the deep absurdity of this ambition if we understand *both* the philosophical theories as philosophy *and* their subsequent history, which is one of failure. This contention about failure, it is important to see, is a contention in both history and philosophy. Rorty finds the inevitable outcome of the philosophical enterprise in the conclusions drawn by Heidegger and Wittgenstein, notably, that a philosophy which properly understands itself will depart from traditional philosophical concerns, abandoning metaphysics and welcoming its replacement by a philosophical therapy which leaves everything as it is, except of course the ambition to philosophize. This conclusion is an outcome in *two* ways, it is both a culmination which can only come at the end of the actual story of philosophy—that is what makes Rorty's thesis historical—and it is a rational culmination, the position which it is logical to hold. We grasp the significance of the story by understanding the philosophical conceptions at its heart, and we arrive at a philosophical conclusion by following the story. In this it is to be distinguished from familiar, but more abstract and ahistorical versions of metaphysical anti-realism. The nature of the metaphysical realism with which Rorty finds fault has emerged over time. It is for this reason that Rorty's thesis, though different in content, is just the sort of thesis Hegel thought he had established at the end of his own endeavours.

What this brief (though I hope accurate) summary demonstrates, is that there is to be found in Rorty's influential work a combination of philosophical and historical elements which are intertwined in precisely the way I argued they have to be intertwined in the history of science. Historical understanding and philosophical illumination can only be satisfactorily achieved if we bring history and philosophy to bear on one another. Such at any rate is the presupposition of Rorty's account of the central problems of philosophy and he is not the only major figure in contemporary philosophy who engages in this kind of endeavour. Alasdair MacIntyre's well known book, *After Virtue*, and its sequels, advance a similarly Hegelian thesis in moral philosophy. According to MacIntyre, contemporary philosophical reflection on ethics takes place at the end of an historical process of cultural fragmentation, and emotivism, for example, is plausible as a philosophical doctrine only because of this history. Understanding the process is crucial both to an adequate account of cultural history and to an analysis of the central problems of modern moral philosophy, but it is an understanding that can be achieved only if we approach the history via the philosophical problems and vice versa. MacIntyre denies that his thesis is Hegelian, because he repudiates any special authority to the end point of the story, that is, the modern period. Nevertheless, his philosophical thesis seems to have authority, if it does, in just this sense; the outcome of his conceptually sophisticated historical investigation enables us to arrive at well-founded judgements on the solutions to philosophical problems proposed at earlier stages. If MacIntyre is right, the theoretical inadequacy of contemporary moral philosophy stems in large part from its historical ignorance.

Rorty and MacIntyre are chosen here as influential contemporary philosophers who can plainly be seen to be engaged in philosophical history. This dimension of MacIntyre's view is one which will be examined more closely in Chapter 5. But there are more general themes in contemporary philosophy which have this character also. Perhaps the most striking example is to be found in the recently fashionable philosophy of postmodernism referred to briefly in Chapter 1. Postmodernist philosophers hold that our understanding of contemporary philosophy, social science and culture in general can only be adequate if we take account of the passing of the presuppositions of the period described as modernity. Chief among these presuppositions is an assumption about the universality of human reason and its power to apprehend reality and prescribe for both theory and practice on the basis of a contextually purified rationality. It is this assumption, postmodernists contend, upon which something frequently referred to as 'the project of the Enlightenment' was built.

The project of the Enlightenment finds its clearest and most prestigious exponent in Immanuel Kant, whose philosophy is rather starkly ahistorical, constructed as it is around a deep distinction between the a priori and the a posteriori, the conceptual and the empirical, the necessary and the contingent. Kant is concerned first and foremost with the necessary structure of the universal human mind, as it shows itself in the theoretical sciences, practical deliberation and aesthetic judgement, the subjects of his three *Critiques*. His peculiar contribution, it is true, is to defend his conception of these forms of reason by *transcendental* argument, as opposed to argument from indubitable first principles, the form of argument that is found in the rationalism of Descartes. That is to say, Kant uses as his foundation not the 'clear and distinct perceptions' to which Cartesians appeal, but the inescapable presuppositions of any mental endeavour on the part of human beings. Yet, according to postmodernist writers, this ahistoric foundationalism is no less of an illusion than the rationalism which preceded it, and only by grasping the essentially historical location of Kant's thought, both in relation to its predecessors and successors, can we understand its contextual nature and hence its limitations. These limitations arise from a misconceived ambition to transcend historical situatedness, which is in fact inherently inescapable. We shall understand the hopelessness of this ambition if we place Kantian philosophy in the historical passage of ideas, a passage which sees the project of Enlightenment arise, develop, fail, and fall.

Many of these themes will be touched upon again in subsequent chapters, and we need not explore this example further here. The point of alluding to it is merely to illustrate that there is in this currently fashionable philosophy the invocation of an historical sequence—premodernity, modernity and postmodernity—which, it is said, illuminates, and hence cannot but be intertwined with, the understanding of philosophical problems. Its existence, and its prominence in modern philosophy, further illustrate the second contention of this chapter, that philosophical history is alive and active in contemporary philosophy.

Even more importantly for present purposes, the philosophy of postmodernism, along with that of Rorty and MacIntyre, attributes a shape to the past. In fact, all these influential approaches can be seen to do so, and to employ some of the very general 'shapes' outlined in Chapter 1. Hegel's philosophy of history, for instance, is progressivist. He sees human understanding as developing by stages from a fragmented and imperfect beginning to the ultimate achievement of perfect unity—which he describes as the Absolute, or Absolute Mind, coming to understand itself. No philosophically well-informed history of science, I imagine, would have much use for any comparable idea of an ultimate and perfect completion in its understanding, a 'Theory of Everything'. For the most part, modern science self-confessedly leaves most questions open and acknowledges, despite its undoubted successes, its own profound ignorance. Yet, as I have outlined it, even science, no less than Hegel, will have a progressivist structure in its own self-understanding, namely a belief, implicit rather than explicit, in scientific experience as the steady abatement of ignorance.

By contrast, Rorty and MacIntyre may be said to be philosophical historians of decline and collapse. The goals of Greek philosophy, on both their accounts, were rational in their day but have subsequently become unstuck. To adhere to the ambitions of a Plato or a Descartes is *now*, but was not *then*, irrational. Judgements of irrationality, therefore, even though they are philosophical judgements, can only be made 'at dusk', and 'dusk' here is to be understood as that grasp of philosophy which is possible only with hindsight. For MacIntyre, the failure of modern philosophy reflects a more general cultural collapse, chiefly in the sphere of the moral. Rorty's view is more properly one of decline—the gradual exhaustion of one sort of intellectual ambition under the power of its own internal misconceptions, though the perception of decline is not to be greeted with despair. The decline of the ambition liberates us, and allows us to endorse the sustaining power of what Michael Oakeshott called the perpetual 'conversation of mankind'.

Progress, decline and collapse are all in my sense 'shapes' of the past, and, as we saw in Chapter 1, shapes that can be found at work in much wider intellectual circles than those of academic philosophy alone. They do not, however, exhaust the possibilities in philosophical history. Equally familiar is the suggestion that the past is to be understood in terms of cycles of cultural growth and decay, a thought to be found amongst the Greeks and brought to greater prominence after Vico, perhaps. Even progress, decline, collapse, and cycle do not comprise an exhaustive list;

religious typology with which (as I earlier observed), grand narrative began, is also important. But the critical examination of progress, decline, and collapse with which the next three chapters are concerned, is the point at which philosophical history proper can really be seen to begin.

The role of analytical philosophy in their examination is, as I have already remarked, one more concerned with structure than with content. That is to say, the main task of philosophical history is to decide how best we are to think of progress and decline as the organizing frameworks of the narratives which empirical investigations into history might complete. Consequently, though it will be necessary in the chapters that follow to consider something of the content of the philosophical histories to which reference is made, it is their conceptual structure which will be the principal focus of interest.

The most useful place to start is with stories of historical progress, partly because in so doing we are inevitably, though not exclusively, beginning with Hegel, the greatest of all philosophical historians. But there are three further reasons. First, progressivism, which reached its zenith in the nineteenth century, has never entirely lost its appeal. Second (as has already been noted), it has recently come to prominence once more, and in an avowedly Hegelian mode, in Fukuyama's *The End of History and the Last Man*. Finally, there is illumination to be found in asking whether the strengths of the progressivist view can be enhanced and its weaknesses reduced by any of the alternatives.

3 Progress

THE last chapter attempted to dispel general doubts about the possibility of philosophical history and the construction of grand narratives. The point of doing so was to set the stage for an exploration of specific types of grand narrative. The first of these is progress, a conception of universal history about which something very general has already been said, but which now needs to be examined in detail.

I

The belief in progress is to be found in most periods (including the present), but it can be said to have reached its height in the nineteenth century where progressivism, as I shall call it, is encountered in thinkers as diverse as Karl Marx and John Stuart Mill (1806–73). The progressivism of the nineteenth century (though not in these two writers) was frequently accompanied by, and often thought to support, additional contentions about the superiority of European culture and the Christian religion, and hence came to be allied with the justification of imperialism. Indeed, in some ways cultural optimism, and a sense of moral superiority are more striking marks of nineteenth-century social thought and practice than the simple belief in historical progress, and it is perhaps these further associated claims of cultural superiority and with them the defence of empire, which have brought progressivism into disrepute in this century, rather than the core historical belief itself.

The reasons for this widespread and highly important change of view are several. First, it is plausible to think that the huge and largely pointless slaughter of the First World War, from the effects of which very few European families escaped, put an end to optimism. There is certainly evidence to support this view when the writings of the first and second decades of this century are compared. Added to this, the subsequent history of the twentieth century with its further wars, the emergence of totalitarianism, the creation of gulags and concentration camps, did little to revive a belief in progress, and perhaps gave grounds for the recurrently popular contention that the world is witnessing a descent into hell. This change in view, from optimism to pessimism, is specially notable in the public attention given in the 1920s and 1930s to the writings of Oswald Spengler, whose *Decline of the West*, one of the most ambitious philosophical histories of the twentieth century (to be considered in more detail in Chapter 6), was published in the aftermath of World War I, for Spengler gives eloquent expression to something of this new found pessimism.

To these considerations we may add the fact that, by about the middle of the twentieth century, all the old colonial empires— the Dutch, the Portuguese, the French, and above all the British —had virtually collapsed. They did so with several important consequential effects upon the cultural self-understanding of those who had established them. With respect to the moral certainties of nineteenth-century progressivism, these effects were twofold. It was under the protection of empire that serious anthropology began. The first anthropologists, such as Sir James Frazer (1854–1941), author of *The Golden Bough*, believed themselves to be investigating and recording the primitive and curious practices of savages. Even before the widespread demise of European empires, the view steadily grew amongst anthropologists that differences between cultures ran too deep to allow simple comparison on a single scale of better and worse, primitive and advanced.

In this way the anthropology which empire had permitted and protected generated a return of the appeal of cultural and ethical relativism, more marked in earlier periods, which in its turn undermined some of the moral basis of imperialism.

Second, both the maintenance of empire and later its collapse caused an important movement of peoples and cultures. The subjects of former colonies slowly, and then more suddenly, congregated in Europe itself. The effect of this movement was to create conditions of cultural pluralism in the heartland of the West. Christianity and the morality of liberal individualism, especially of the more 'muscular' North European variety, simply ceased to be the cultural monolith in the countries where it originated. The claims of Islam to be a distinctive and important cultural voice in several European societies, for instance, cannot now be ignored, not so much because of the moral or intellectual challenge they present to the universalistic aspirations of Christian theology and morality, a challenge felt in Europe as early as the middle of the sixteenth century,[1] but more simply because of the effect of the social presence in Christian Europe of large numbers of Far and Middle-Eastern Muslims for whom contemporary Christianity is an alien religion.

Finally, progressivism, which is ultimately an historical view, became the object of a sustained attack from within, so to speak. It was the historian Herbert Butterfield who first identified and then discredited 'the Whig interpretation of history'. According to this 'Whig interpretation', historical events are to be understood as encounters between the forces of progress and the forces of reaction. Thus the Renaissance and the Reformation represent 'advances', against which such things as the Counter-Reformation are reactions. Butterfield attacks this sort of history of the rise of Protestantism, claiming that the very language of 'Reformation'

---

[1] The Koran was translated into English in 1649 and into Italian about 100 years earlier.

and 'Counter-Reformation' embodies the contentious Whig interpretation, and hence cannot be made to bear it out. He argues,
on the contrary, for the importance of understanding Luther and
other reformers in the terms of their own time and their own
conceptions. His is, so to speak, an early version of contextual-
ism, the principal force of which is to cast doubt upon history
written from the point of view of the concerns of the present.
Against this, Butterfield's view of good history requires historians to set aside the preconceptions and concerns of their own
time and to understand the past in *its* terms. This ideal of historical writing is one that many historians have come to share,
and their doing so has contributed still further to diminishing
the attractions of the Whiggish concern with progress, not just
among their own number, but more widely as well.

Together these somewhat different, if interconnected, lines of
thought have combined in the minds of many to relegate full-
blooded historical progressivism to the status of an intellectual
curiosity. This relegation, however, has at least some things to be
regretted about it, for it has caused the strengths and attractions
of progressivism to be overlooked. But intellectual relegation of
this sort is never likely to be permanent, because progressivism,
along with some of the other simple grand narratives we will
consider, has perennial appeal. And in fact, the publication in 1992
of Francis Fukuyama's *End of History*, which will be discussed
later in this chapter, together with the attention it attracted, is
evidence that it is possible to expound a serious historical progressivism once more.

No doubt there was a certain naïve (if to my mind admirable)
optimism in the Victorian period, but to appreciate its real
strengths, we need to recognize at the outset that the belief in
progress does not have to be unwarrantedly optimistic. This is
more readily apparent if we distinguish the belief in progress as
such from the beliefs about the moral and religious superiority
of Europe associated with it in the nineteenth century. Once this

distinction is made, an argument can be advanced to show just how difficult it is to avoid some sort of progressivism. A large part of contemporary resistance to nineteenth-century progressivism is itself moral, the expression of moral distaste for a view which seems to warrant the denigration (and perhaps coercive suppression) of alternative cultural and religious forms. However, it is hard to resist the implication that modern views which accord with this distaste, and which share the accompanying toleration of cultural variety it is generally thought to promote and justify, are for this reason better, an advance on earlier more parochial ways of thinking. But if they are *better* ways of thinking about other cultures, then presumably some progress in human understanding has been made. Modern cultural relativists cannot but think their view an improvement on the narrower moral thinking of the past. If so, however, progressivism re-enters our understanding of history.

There may appear to be some sleight-of-hand about this argument, and though I believe it to be a good one, there are indeed plausible responses to be made to it. Still, whatever the truth about this, progressivism need not rest its case here. Nor need it be concerned with the contentious sphere of the moral at all, since it does not have to maintain that progress has been made in every sphere of human endeavour. Serious doubts about whether the religion and morality of the West, even in their modern tolerant forms, set the pattern that all must ultimately follow are consistent with the more modest belief that with respect to *some* aspects of human existence, the past is a story of progress from worse to better. And indeed, though it is possible to acknowledge some progress without being a 'progressivist', with respect to certain aspects, technological and economic change for instance, some sort of progressivism is hard to resist. The followers of Bacon in the seventeenth century believed themselves to be on the verge of a complete mastery of nature. In this they were overly optimistic, but even on a superficial reading of history, they were right to see themselves as part of a process which, in terms of knowledge and resources, has resulted in human beings in general being better equipped to ameliorate the human condition now than a hundred years ago, and better then than two hundred years before that. A similar initial plausibility attaches to a progressivist account of industrial development and the treatment of illness. Technology, prosperity, and medicine, of course, are just three (importantly related) aspects of human life and though a broadly materialist progressivism might remain silent on further aspects, such as art, politics, and morality, sooner or later these need to be considered before we could conclude that there is a sufficiently large picture of cultural progress to warrant the claims of progressivism to be a 'universal history'. But for the moment the exploration of conceptual structure can usefully begin on this more limited ground.

As a final preliminary point, we should note that progressivism does not have to invoke anything in the way of a teleology, or grand *design*. Nor need it appeal to any hidden agent or to forces of inevitability. Initially, at any rate, it can be construed merely as a descriptive summary of the past—that across human history there is a perceptible, recountable, steady progress from worse to better. It is in this version that considerable strengths and attractions lie, and since it is still a view that lends a distinctive shape to the narrative of the past, it is thus one possible philosophical history.

Even of this relatively straightforward belief about technology, economics, and medicine, however, whatever its immediate plausibility, we must ask 'Is it true?'. In deciding how such a comparatively simple question should be answered, philosophical history of a more sophisticated sort comes into play. For instance, we might suppose that the simple version of progressivism is nothing more complex than an empirical hypothesis about technology and medicine, one that must answer to historical fact. To an extent this is certainly correct. Being a belief about the contingent course of history, it must accord with such evidence as we have. Nevertheless, as we saw in the first chapter, its being a *world* history makes the number of facts potentially relevant to it enormous, even when, as for the moment we have restricted ourselves to only some aspects of existence. This means, at the very least, that there is preliminary work to be done in deciding how the evidence is most properly marshalled.

As the exploration of this apparently preliminary considera-tion proceeds, it will become clear that a complex set of further questions cannot but arise, questions involving central philo-sophical issues about human values and their transhistorical assessment. These questions take their significance here, how-ever, from a substantive interest in the past, 'Is historical pro-gressivism true?', and this in turn illustrates the central contention of the last chapter, that a sharp division between historical and philosophical investigation loses most of its usefulness when we give serious attention to claims about the shape of the past.

II

Our concern is with progress, then. Any belief in progress, not just of progress in history, might be thought at first sight to require two distinct elements: (1) a descriptive account of some sequence, and (2) a principle of evaluation by which this is to be assessed as involving changes for better or worse. If this simple analysis of the idea of progress were correct, it would imply that the two elements are logically independent of each other in this sense: someone could agree with the facts as recounted, and at the same time deny that they amount to progress. This fits with the view that some people have taken of economic development; they agree that the world is richer, but not that it is better off. However, the supposition of logical independence cannot be cor-rect. In order to establish that in some sequence there has been progress, we must not only invoke a principle of evaluation, but also show that the principle invoked has continuous application to the beginning and end of the sequence. And whether it has or not is a matter that depends on the contents of sequence recorded. Thus, the applicability of the principle of evaluation is an important part of the accepted record, so that to accept the latter implies at least partial acceptance of the former.

To see this, consider a more simple case than that of a grand historical narrative. Suppose someone claims that athletic performances have improved over a given period and employs the not implausible standard of faster times. If, as a matter of record, faster times have been a feature of later stages in the period under review, and faster times are what interest us, we can claim that there has been change for the better. But to claim that there has been *progress* we need also to show that the athletes whose performances are being judged were themselves working to this standard. If for instance they were striving for greater distances, and though they ran the same distances more quickly, the distances they were able to sustain were not much longer, they would not have regarded themselves as having made progress in their endeavours, and hence cannot be said by contemporary athletes to have done so. This does not mean that we are wrong to commend them for faster times from a modern point of view, or regard them as successful by our standards. We could even coherently criticize them for their choice of the wrong goal. But we still cannot describe the athletic history which connects their activity to ours as one of progress.

Similarly, if, to take a more ambitious example, we claim that between, say, the school system of the Middle Ages and that of the present time there has been a progressive development, we shall have to show, not only that there have been schools throughout that period and that, by our standards, present-day schools are measurably better, but that the standards we employ also apply to the schools of the Middle Ages in the sense that the educational goals of those schools were such as would permit them to recognize present-day schools as more effective in achieving those goals. Suppose the aim of the schoolmasters of the Middle Ages was to instil in their pupils a greater knowledge of the Christian religion. It could be the case that as a result of their endeavours, significant impetus was lent to the extension of literacy and general understanding, as a consequence of which literacy rates today vastly exceed anything that could have been expected then. But if, at the same time, knowledge of the Christian religion has not been extended, or has even diminished, the educational attainments of the present, to which we attach great value, will not have value from their point of view. It is thus essential, wherever a judgement of progress (as opposed to change thought to be for the better) is made, that the values and principles invoked are applicable to all the stages over which progress is said to have been made. And this further condition, of course, itself requires historical establishment, since what the goals of past historical agents were is in large part a matter for historical inquiry.

What these examples illustrate is that the two elements which the concept of progress requires, namely the record of events and the principle of evaluation, though they can usefully be distinguished, cannot be wholly independent. Any principle capable of generating judgements of progress must be shown to be historically relevant to the period about which the judgement is made. It is evidently wrong to criticize mediaeval monasteries for not being comprehensive schools if they never tried to be such. The application of a wholly independent (but inevitably wholly modern) principle of evaluation would lead in fact to the sort of 'apriorism' discussed in the last chapter, an apriorism of which, it has been widely thought, nineteenth-century writers were guilty, and which has tended to give progressivism in general a bad name. But it is important to stress that it would be equally mistaken to fall into an historical relativism by simply assuming the validity of the standards people in the past set for themselves. It is both possible and legitimate to criticize early schools for having limited educational objectives, and the limitedness of those objectives will be demonstrated by developing conceptions of education which of necessity make their appearance at a later point in the sequence. Once again, there is nothing peculiar here about the historical case. In assessing my progress at the piano, for instance, it would be absurd to condemn my early efforts for failing to be those of a concert pianist, but it would be equally wrong to rest content with them just because they measured up reasonably well to standards appropriate to that stage. What this shows is that judgements of progress have to employ a reflective dialogue, so to speak, between the historical record and the evaluative notions employed such that *two* conditions are met. We must escape slavish adherence to the conventional values of particular places or periods (which is the error to which relativism is prone), while at the same time ensuring that the standards of judgement and values employed do not appear from some abstract Olympian height (which is the error of apriorism). Rather, the standards and values employed in a judgement of progress must themselves be explained and defended in terms relevant to the periods under consideration.

However, this explanatory connection may be made at some remove—the standards and values we invoke in our judgements of progress may be implicit rather than explicit in earlier periods, as for instance in the parallel drawn with learning the piano. There is more to be said about this last possibility, but for the moment it is sufficient to observe that there is a greater complexity in the conceptual structure of progress than in the simple two-element, description/evaluation, model with which we began. Although we are still working here with the limited idea of material progress, further complication arises in connection with the move required for the generation of a more general history from judgements of progress in just one aspect of human existence, to the belief in progress overall.

There are two important ways in which this move may become problematic. First, judgements of progress in one respect may be offset (or at least thought to be offset) by placing them in a larger context. For example, we might agree that modern armaments constitute a huge improvement on earlier weapons in terms of accuracy and efficiency. But if the effect of this improvement is that more people get killed or injured, we might none the less deny that the improvement constituted overall progress in welfare. Second, though this is a more important issue as we move beyond the purely material, it seems that some aspects of human life are more significant than others from the point of view of human existence taken as a whole. For instance, from the scanty evidence available, it appears that the mode of life of North American Indians changed very little over a period of 12,000 years or so. Their social structures, technology, and religion during that time, so far as we can tell, exhibit little or nothing that could be called development. Suppose for the sake of argument that this is true. Were we now to discover that during this same period there was a recordable development in the games North American Indians played, and that these developed, let us imagine, from simple pastimes to major social events which called forth very considerable physical skill and strategic sophistication, there would still be a question whether the conclusion that their civilization had progressed could be justified. Part of the reason seems to be that in comparison with domestic technology, methods of production, and social and commercial arrangements, games are not central enough to human life. Had evidence emerged that these other features of the lives of North American Indians had developed greatly, it would be much more plausible to describe their civilization as having progressed, and it would continue to be so even if their games showed no very marked improvement. It follows that before we can decide the question of *universal* progress in the sense of progress overall, we must not only be able to record specific aspects of a culture in which progress has been made, but must also form some estimation of the relative importance of these various aspects. Without this further step, the question whether the progress detected amounts to progress overall cannot be resolved.

Yet one more important difficulty must also be noted at this stage. It arises once a further step, essential to progressivism, is made, the step not just from progress in one aspect to progress overall within one culture, but from progress within cultures to progress in human history. In the elaboration and defence of progressivism, it very evidently matters a great deal which parts of the world and its history we look at, and just whose progress is under consideration. For example, suppose we restrict our attention to economic progress. It is plausible to think that most upper-class ancient Romans were better off than most present-day inhabitants of Mali or Mozambique, and hence that some current conditions are economically worse than some obtaining in the past. Is the truth of this sufficient to show that humanity has not progressed? Or should we rather restrict our comparisons, and hence our claims, to specific groups or classes of people, modern with ancient Romans, former with present Malians, say? But if restrictions of this sort are required, how do we determine when we really are comparing like with like? The suggestion just canvassed takes national groupings as the base comparison. What reason is there to do this, as opposed, for instance, to comparing occupational groups? An alternative, one might imagine, would consist in a general averaging of present and past prosperity. 'On average', someone may say, 'people are better off, better educated, longer living, and so on, now than they have ever been.' But the empirical difficulties facing such an alternative seem to be insuperable. We can scarcely arrive at averages for these things for the present day (leaving aside the additional problems of averaging dimensions such as educational standing), and cannot make even the roughest of estimates of them in the past for any but small parts of the globe, and even those for very limited periods of time.

These complications do not exhaust the problems which any serious progressivism must face, but they are, it seems to me, amongst the most important. In the face of them, it is tempting to think that any attempt to establish that human history is a story of progress is hopeless. But this is too pessimistic. The problems just enumerated arise from the fact that we have not as yet discovered a way of *stating* the belief in progress which will enable us to relate the different dimensions of value, and this prevents us from structuring such evidence as we possess. In the next section therefore, the principal task will be to find a way of stating this belief which, if it does not completely resolve, at least removes a great deal of the force in the difficulties we have encountered.

III

Progress implies both change and improvement. Furthermore, as I argued above, the standard by which improvement is to be judged is one which must be applicable to the whole period of the change. These points may be further illustrated by a simple example of undoubted progress—methods of lighting. The electric lamp is an improvement upon the gas mantle, which in its turn is an improvement on the oil lamp, and so on back to burning torches. In the matter of lighting, therefore, it seems uncontentious to claim that there has been change and improvement. But there has also been progress, because the standard by which recordable changes are judged to be improvements is one which we have reason to think can be applied continuously, even over the rather long period to which the claim refers. The purposes which we may suppose burning torches were intended to serve are the same as those which are better served by each new method of lighting in the sequence. Thus, in claiming that the invention of electric light introduces a real improvement, we need not be presupposing anything illicit about the world of long ago, and in all probability are not in fact doing so. The assumption at work is only that ancient people wished for light for much the same reason as we do today—to see in the absence of natural light—and that they recognized the troublesome inefficiency of rush torches to this end as much as we would recognize it. This assumption may not hold of every candidate for technological progress. Aeroplanes, for example, dramatically reduced the amount of time and the discomfort involved in crossing the Atlantic, but there is at least some question whether they are in this respect an improvement on, say, the coracle whose purpose, it may be, was never to make such long journeys (though of course relatively early ships, such as Viking longships, did make ambitious journeys). If we are serious about the belief in progress from stone age to space age, we must be careful not to beg the question by presupposing that those things which *we* find useful and hence admire are, in virtue of that fact, to be declared progressive developments for humanity as a whole. Our judgements of progress, we might say, must not be 'epochocentric'. Still, the lighting example shows that such judgements are in principle possible.

What is needed is some way in which epochocentricity can be circumvented. In order to ensure that a general estimate of progress accords with the logical requirements discussed earlier as satisfactorily as does the example of lighting, we need to postulate some general equivalent of the fixed point of reference given by the specific purpose of lighting. One way of doing this is to invoke the concepts of human nature and the human condition. We can, that is to say, conceive of history as the story of the efforts of humankind to cope with the facts of the human condition—the scarcity of resources, the existence of disease, the possibility of injury, the certainty of death, and so on—against the background of the abiding requirements of human nature. In this way it is possible to view human experience as an encounter between relatively fixed sets of abilities, aptitudes, needs, desires, etc. (human nature), and an environment in which they have their working out (the human condition). For example, human beings must eat and stay warm. They can only do these things in certain ways and only certain of the items in the world in which they find themselves will satisfy these needs. Their physiology dictates what they need by way of nourishment and warmth, and their psychology further constrains them. The natural world on the other hand has given to only certain items in the world the properties of satisfying those needs. Stones are not bread, scorpions are not fish, and these are facts about the human condition. The two are not wholly independent of course. Our ability to manipulate the world increases the world's capacity to satisfy our needs. We can grow food as well as find it, raise animals as well as hunt them. The general point, however, is that human nature has its constant desires and needs, and these can be made to serve as a common referent for both stone age and space age. The question of progress then becomes a question of whether these needs and desires have been better met as time has passed.

Philosophers and other theorists have not infrequently denied that there is any constant nature of this sort. This is a point to which it will be necessary to return, but for the moment I shall assume that there is. If so, it is reasonably plain how the concept of human nature determines which aspects of human experience are pertinent to the question of progress, because it will only be those methods of manipulating the environment to meet the ends of health, survival, desire satisfaction, and procreation that will be relevant. All these allow, certainly, for a substantial difference of opinion about just what is to be included. For example, whereas food production, longevity, disease control, amount of leisure time, and other such things have an obvious place in the estimation of progress on this account, it is disputable whether, and how, increases in knowledge or artistic sophistication might figure in it. Are they to be regarded chiefly as means to more material ends, means whose usefulness the forces of natural evolution determine, perhaps, or are they rather objects of independent human desires, having become so possibly as a sort of 'spin-off' from evolutionary forces?

Answers to this question are difficult to arrive at, but it is worth noting here that these aspects of human experience might more easily be accommodated in a general estimation of progress if we adopted a similar, though alternative strategy, in which the procedure is reversed, and a conception of the human condition is held constant and inquiry made instead into the changing nature of human beings. Here the question becomes: Given the constant facts of hunger, sex, disease, the transience of human life, and above all, death, is there greater grace or spirit in the response of human beings over the ages? Is there, for instance, any demonstrable increase in the artistic sensitivity with which the human condition is portrayed and understood? Is modern religion more ennobling than the religions of old, signalled in the move from the manipulative aspirations of magic to spiritual acceptance, perhaps? It is plain that these alternative strategies might yield contrary results. There is no a-priori reason to think that if the lot of human beings has improved almost immeasurably from the point of view of diet, health, longevity, and so on, there must at the same time have been a similar improvement in their response to it. Adversity is sometimes ennobling, and conversely opulence is not infrequently corrupting or degrading. Consequently the choice of strategy would seem extremely important for the investigation with which we are here concerned.

However, this possibility of contrary results raises a further question. Can these really be alternative strategies for progressivism? Might not a convincing version of the belief in progress require that both of them be adopted, and that both of them return a positive result? This is an issue which we will have to consider further. For immediate purposes, however, it is enough to have shown that by employing the concepts of human nature and the human condition it is possible to formulate a clearer idea of what the belief in progress amounts to and how we might inquire into its truth. There is a possible constant against which the changes which history records can be measured, and since we can continue to restrict ourselves to material progress, we can make a start by concentrating on the first method of employing this constant, that is to say, on the suggestion that the human condition has improved over time such that human welfare is at a higher level nowadays than it has ever been.

This version of progressivism may be said, broadly, to invoke an Aristotelian conception of progress. Aristotle's moral philosophy is built upon the idea of human flourishing. By his account (a typically Greek one), human beings, in common with most other beings, have a *telos* or intrinsic nature. In the light of this nature, certain modes of existence can be determined to be better or worse for each kind of thing. Thus, the growing conditions of a plant can be determined as better or worse for the plant, given its nature. Some plants flourish in dry conditions and sicken in wet conditions, and vice versa for others. It is somewhat contentious, certainly, to extend this conception of nature or *telos* to human beings, but if we do so, it does not take much further innovation to give the general conception an historical dimension. We need only ask whether, given the *telos* of human beings, the possibility of their flourishing has increased as time has passed, whether, that is to say, human life has become better.

An obvious question arises at once. Better for whom? As I remarked earlier, such a suggestion is complicated by the possibility of different group comparisons. To improvise upon a previous example, there is every reason to think that the lot of, for instance, eighteenth-century Glasgow merchants was considerably better than that of present-day beggars on the streets of Calcutta, and that the disruption of peace during the English Civil War was, for the ordinary Englishman, not nearly so devastating as the twentieth-century civil war in Lebanon was for the inhabitants of Beirut. We need to know, therefore, from what point of view the judgement of progress is to be made. Remarks about 'Mankind' or 'Humanity' having done this or that tend to disguise the essential place of the individual in the estimation of progress. On the face of it, it is small comfort to poverty-stricken peasants, no better and possibly worse off than their forebears, to know that someone else is better off than *his* forebears were, even if this 'someone else' is taken to be the representative of 'Mankind'. In short, what is needed is an appropriately impersonal standpoint from which the merits of different ages, nations, classes, and occupations may be judged. This impartial standpoint must thus have two essential features—it must not presuppose the preferences of any one age or the membership of any particular economic or other grouping.

IV

The crucial question is how to describe such a standpoint. The approach I propose to adopt employs an old philosophical device, that of an Impartial Observer. We can simply build into this device the properties that are to be attributed to human nature. Of course, the idea of human nature, and hence the idea of an Impartial Observer possessed of just that nature, require a considerable measure of abstraction and idealization. But there is nothing inherently objectionable in this. Gardening books, for example, happily recommend standard regimes for chrysanthemums or roses, while freely acknowledging that individual specimens will always be more or less true to type.

The Impartial Observer (IO) becomes an adjudicator between different periods and places by exercising preferences between various possible conditions of existence, based upon his nature as a human being. These judgements become historically relevant when the preferences range over not merely possible conditions, but those which were actual at different times and places in the past. In other words, IOs have a strictly *human* nature, one that is in no way cultivated by the practices or preferences of any given age, class or civilization. As a result, their preference for one age or society rather than another may be said to be a purely human preference, and hence can be regarded as an impartial preference between alternative points in human history.

By employing this device, it is now possible to state a fairly concise and rigorous version of the belief in historical progress. To be more precise, it is possible to state a number of related, though different hypotheses. Only some of these are relevant for present purposes. In fact just three such formulae will exhibit the underlying structure of this interpretation of progressivism. Consider first this contention:

1. Up to the present time, for any time, there is a time later than that time at which an Impartial Observer would have preferred to live; at any time up to the present this could have been said truly.

A formulation of this kind overcomes the problem of relevant group comparisons. This is because it supposes that the IO is offered a choice of when it would be preferable to live, and being possessed only of a universal human nature, is unconstrained by limitations of occupation, nationality, social position and so on. The IO can thus express a preference for any social position, and can thus compare the best position at any point in the past, wherever it is to be obtained, with the best position, again anywhere, at any later time. And what the formula says is that, compared with any point in the past, the IO will always find a later, preferable, point. As stated, however, this first formulation is a strictly linear conception of progress. Since it says that at *any* time in the past it could have been said that there is a later preferable time, it amounts to the hypothesis that progress has been continuous, and its direction constant. It may thus be represented graphically as in Fig. 1.

Now neither of these claims seems very plausible as a matter of historical fact. We have good reason to believe that on any

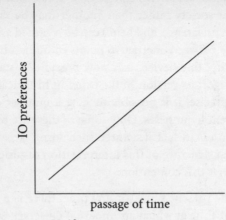

FIG. 1. Uniform progress

dimension—economic, medical, political, artistic—history has had its share of downs as well as ups. This means that there will be points in the past, when history underwent a temporary decline, where it would not have been true to say that there was a later time at which the IO would have preferred to live. If so, it follows that any plausible belief in progress must allow that the rate of progress has been variable. As a result the true picture of progress is much more likely to be as in Fig. 2. The difference between this view, which we might call a postulation of evolutionary progress, and the more simple linear view may be expressed in the following formula:

2. Up to the present time, for any time, there is a later time at which an Impartial Observer would have preferred to live; but this could *not* have been said truly at every time up to the present.

Even this revised formula is not quite sufficient to capture the most plausible picture of progress, because as it stands it cannot be distinguished from a belief in what might be called

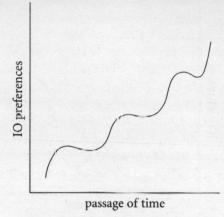

passage of time

Fig. 2. Evolutionary progress

revolutionary progress (which is, I think, the view Kant espouses in *The Idea of a Universal History*). This may be pictured as in Fig. 3. Revolutionary progress can be distinguished from evolutionary progress as represented in Fig. 2, by the following formula:

3. Up to the present time, for any time, there is a later time at which an Impartial Observer would have preferred to live, but this could not have been said truly at every time, and between most times in the past an Impartial Observer would have been indifferent.

Taking this possibility into account, the formula which best expresses the most plausible form of progressivism, the belief in evolutionary progress (Fig. 2), is this.

4. Up to the present time, for any time, there is a later time at which an Impartial Observer would have preferred to live. This could have been said truly at the majority of past times, but not at every time.

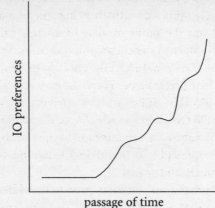

FIG. 3. Revolutionary progress

In arriving at this formula I have merely asserted the greater plausibility of evolutionary over either linear or revolutionary conceptions of progress. But this is not an assertion of any great moment. What any of these formulae shows is that the belief in progress can, despite its universal scope, be given an expression which renders it an empirically testable hypothesis. Moreover, the test is one of falsification, which sets to rest many of the Popperian doubts discussed in Chapter 2. We have only to locate some time in the past, in any social or economic position, which from the point of view of the Impartial Observer is to be preferred to any later time, and we will thereby have refuted the progressivist's hypothesis. Alternatively, and perhaps more interestingly, it is enough if we can locate a time compared with which no later time is preferable. By this method we have reduced the amount of evidence we have to handle to entirely manageable proportions, and converted an ambitious thesis about the shape of the past into one answerable to the facts historical inquiry uncovers.

If all this seems too easy, it is perhaps because certain central questions have been set to one side. Most crucially, the method adopted here to bring precise form to the belief in progress depends entirely upon our actually being able to make sufficient judgements from the point of view of an Impartial Observer. This possibility in turn depends upon our being able to characterize the Observer's nature fully enough to generate a wide enough range of preferences. There are two ways in which we might fail to do this. Either we can attribute no nature whatever to Impartial Observers, in which case they will have no preferences, or the nature we can attribute to them is so very limited that they must be held to be indifferent between a large number of historical times and places.

Both these suggestions certainly need to be addressed, but the first of them—that we can attribute no human nature whatever to the IO— seems to me implausible. At the very least, since we can say of all human beings that, *ceteris paribus,* they will want to eat, will want to avoid starvation, cold, and danger, we can attribute these wants to Impartial Observers. Consequently, we can assert, once again other things being equal, that they will prefer any time at which they are well fed, warm, and safe, to any at which they are not, and that from a strictly human point of view there has been progress if it is true that we can always find a point later in time at which these wants are better satisfied. However, the second objection has more substance to it, because it is obvious that this limited version of the belief in progress is in fact false. If this is *all* we could say of the Impartial Observer's nature, we would have insufficient grounds for asserting that human history shows a progressive development. There is plainly a very large number of times and places in the past which the Impartial Observer could occupy and at which there is the possibility of being equally well fed, equally warm, and equally safe. Without taking into account the wider dimensions of science, the arts, political freedom, and so on, we have little ground for supposing anything other than indifference between most ages on the part of Impartial Observers.

This does not quite put an end to progressivism of the limited material variety. It might still be claimed that in the material sense there has been progress because, compared with earlier times there are at later times *more* positions that IO's would prefer. This is, I think, the idea that the talk of averaging canvassed briefly at an earlier stage was aiming to capture, and many of the same problems will arise here too. But even if they could be overcome, the resulting progressivism would fall far short of that which has generally found favour, for it would be silent on the social, moral, and political progress of humankind.

What is needed then, is some defence of the idea that we can reasonably attribute to the IO a fairly wide range of (amongst others) political, moral, educational, and artistic preferences, while remaining socially uncontaminated and thus strictly human, and this does not seem a very promising task. Of course we cannot assert a priori that any attempt to describe the nature of the Impartial Observer, i.e. human nature, must produce relatively sparse economic/material results, but it is a real question whether the general Aristotelian structure with which we have been working is likely to produce anything much better. And an even more telling question is whether, even if it could be made to do so, a very much fuller account would adequately serve the ends of progressivism. To decide both these questions we need to ask how it might be arrived at.

V

Before turning to this issue, however, it is perhaps worth noting that the most celebrated recent attempt to defend the merits of a progressivist philosophy of history, namely Fukuyama's *The End of History and the Last Man*, can be interpreted as having this essentially Aristotelian structure (somewhat contrary to its own claims to be Hegelian as interpreted by Kojeve). Fukuyama self-consciously employs the concept of human nature and it has, he thinks, two important dimensions. The first is the economic, by which we may understand the range of material needs and desires human beings have, the sorts of things which formed the basis of the IO's preference in the thought experiment with which we have just been engaged. This material dimension explains not only the development of systems of production, but the development of science, which provides human beings with unparalleled assistance in the expansion of economic prosperity. But Fukuyama attempts to construe human nature in broader terms also. By his account, human beings have an aspect to their essential nature which he describes with the Greek word *thymos*, that is, the psychological need for recognition. It is this second dimension which provides the dominant driving force behind changes in social forms and political organization, as opposed to changes in productive techniques and means of material satisfaction, and it is in terms of their capacity to satisfy *thymos* by which the respective merits of such forms are to be judged. Indeed Fukuyama expressly claims that "Marxism, 'modernisation theory', or any other theory of history based primarily on economics will be radically incomplete unless it takes account of the thymotic part of the soul, and of the struggle for recognition as a major driver of history" (*End of History*, pp. 204–5). The centrality of *thymos* explains, in his view, the prominence of nationalistic feeling and its somewhat surprising, and certainly striking ability to dominate, even exclude, concern with economic well-being, although he also argues that ultimately this need for recognition endorses the superiority of democratic liberalism over more narrow forms of nationalism.

Fukuyama's theoretical accommodation of several unquestionably important strands of modern history lends great strength to his analysis, and indeed it is difficult to summarize such a highly informed and imaginative book in a few paragraphs. But at the heart of his thesis are two claims: that the material desires which form so substantial a part of human nature are best served by scientific advance and economic freedom, and that the equally basic human desire for recognition from and amongst one's fellows, together with what we might call moral self-mastery, meets its greatest satisfaction in liberal democracy, which is marked both by the belief in economic freedom and an emphasis on the political equality of all. Thus, capitalist, liberal democratic society is that which best fits human nature. Other social forms either rely upon the domination of just one group of people or social subset—the various forms of fascism, say—or like socialism, they give exclusive prominence to equality at the expense of prosperity. This special fittedness to human nature explains both the initial historical emergence of liberal democracy and the subsequent convergence of a desire for it on the part of almost all human beings, a convergence which is all the more notable and significant because it draws together people from vastly different historical traditions.

The crucial role of this twofold basis of desire is, according to Fukuyama, most clearly evidenced of late by the collapse of socialism and the manifest aspiration in almost every part of the globe to something like Western, especially American, economic and political structure. This form of social organization, being marked out as it is by its economic freedom, political equality and democratic government, is in a strong sense *naturally* preferable; it best realizes the fundamental nature of human beings. This is what makes it more stable than either charismatic autocracy or visionary egalitarianism, its two most prominent rivals, of which historical exemplars abound. It is this connection with human nature which carries the implication with which both Hegel, and now Fukuyama have been specially associated, namely that the arrival of political and economic liberalism marks the end of history, not in the ludicrous sense (which some critics have foolishly imputed to him) that henceforth nothing will happen, but in the sense that no further major development in formations of human society is required, and hence none is to be expected.

Since the driving forces of history are most adequately accommodated in capitalist liberal democratic society, there is nowhere left for them to drive to.

Fukuyama presents a subtle version of progressivism and makes an impressive case in its defence. Like many philosophical historians, however, he lends too much weight, perhaps, to a very limited period of history. The true significance of the collapse of communism in Eastern Europe, on which he lays great store, may only be ascertainable with the passage of a greater length of time than he has allowed. My aim here, however, is not to examine closely the merits of his case, but to note that the structure of his theory fits that with which I have so far been concerned. It judges progress from the point of view of a universal human nature, one shared by peoples of every time and place. In my terms, Impartial Observers, according to Fukuyama, have reason to prefer recent social and political organization because it more adequately fits the structure of the economic and thymotic desires which comprise their nature. It is thus an Aristotelian conception.

Fukuyama himself believes his theory to be Hegelian, and of course there is something to be said for the view that anyone who advances a theory of history according to which the past is coherent and directional is to that degree following in the footsteps of Hegel. Nevertheless there is an important distinction to be drawn between Hegelian and Aristotelian conceptions of progress, which now needs to be made explicit.

VI

The consideration of Fukuyama's philosophy of history has not advanced the argument from the point it reached at the end of the preceding section. Rather it serves to illustrate the basic structure of an Aristotelian conception, and to show that it has been put to effective use in recent times. But we have still to ask about its general adequacy. Aristotle's idea of human nature may be described as a biological one, and with the discrediting of Greek biology some centuries ago, it fell into disfavour. In the last twenty years or so, however, Aristotelian biology, or rather the Aristotelian/biological approach to moral philosophy, has undergone something of a revival. The best known recent work of this sort is Mary Midgley's *Beast and Man*. Midgley's book is Aristotelian in conception, but not in content. Its content comes in large part from ethological rather than strictly biological studies, studies such as those of Konrad Lorenz, for instance, and what it purports to offer (or at least to show what is on offer) is an account of the nature of human beings which will enable us to discern what things are human excellences. The idea is that empirical ethology gives us an account of human nature which goes beyond the physiological, which is to say, an account of the nature of humans as a distinct species of animal. It is from this broadly animal nature, Midgley and others contend, that we can derive an account of human flourishing, or in older language, 'the good for man'.

The picture of human nature that emerges from ethology is of course a much fuller one than the paltry sketch offered in a preceding section and it is fairly plain how it might be made to assist us in the question of progress. If with the aid of ethology we can construct a more comprehensive account of the nature of human beings, of which the IO is the perfect representative in my scheme of things, and thus determine 'the good for man', the IO will prefer any place in any age in which human flourishing is more fully realizable. But will this fuller account in its turn give us a clear measure of progress? Will a time preferred by the IO on this basis be a progressive development on any earlier time?

There are at least two reasons for thinking that the conception of progress with which we have been working so far cannot in fact do this, and its deficiency in this respect must lead on to a more Hegelian notion. The first of these is rather obvious. Progress implies change for the better, movement towards the good. On the Aristotelian account this turns out to be the good for man, and we can thus invoke the naturalistic fallacy, made famous by G. E. Moore. This is the fallacy of supposing that any natural property, in this case human flourishing, can be identified with the good, since it is always intelligible to question the goodness of a natural property. In other words, even if ethology provides us with a clear and full account of what is good for human beings, we can always ask whether what is good for human beings is good *simpliciter*. Any view, such as that formulated by orthodox Christianity according to which human nature is fallen and without redemption naturally seeks evil, would deny the validity of just such an inference. This is a very important question, but it is not one on which I am going to dwell, because whether the naturalistic fallacy can be invoked in this way is a highly contentious matter. Midgley, for one, argues that any argument that employs the naturalistic fallacy at this point is itself fallacious, and many have claimed that the idea of 'good *simpliciter*' is incoherent. For this reason I shall concentrate on problems that arise elsewhere.

Strictly, if we are working with the Aristotelian conception, we cannot give any clear examples of progress in the absence of at least some outline conception of our animal nature and hence of the preferences of the Impartial Observer. However, we are free to imagine what they will be like and make plausible guesses even where our knowledge of human nature, in the relevant sense, is sketchy. To see this we only have to go back to the example of methods of lighting. In this case, I argued, it makes perfectly good sense to claim that there has been progress because we may reasonably suppose that the purpose for which rush torches were intended is the very same as that which electric light serves better—namely, to see in the absence of natural light. That this is in the strongest sense a *natural* preference of human beings, in the same way that avoiding pain or hunger is, is implausible no doubt, but it is not implausible to suppose that the usefulness of being able to see in the absence of natural light can easily be connected with desires which are natural in the Aristotelian sense, though we cannot actually make this connection, however, until we have a suitably full account of human nature.

However, the structure of progress on this conception is clear. There is an identifiable, universal human end and it is better served as time passes and history proceeds. The second problem mentioned at the end of Section V—can such a conception best serve the purposes of progressivism?—now arises, and can be stated more succinctly: do the most plausible candidates for progressive development through history have this structure?

VII

It will be instructive to return here to the case of science, discussed at some length in the last chapter. The most cursory examination of the pre-Socratic fragments shows that there is in what is called early Greek 'science' no very clear distinction between physics, astronomy, philosophy, mathematics, and divinity. The early Greeks, or a few of them at any rate, pursued inquiries, which there is some reason to call 'scientific' but the aim and nature of which were rather cloudy. If science has progressed since that time, which it evidently seems to have done, then given the cloudiness of these early aims, it cannot be a simple matter of its achieving the ends of the early Greeks better. Rather, those ends themselves have been refined, and 'fulfilling them better' must be taken to include this refinement. In other words, though there has been progress, the original ends cannot be thought to be fixed, as the Aristotelian conception requires. At the same time, it would be wrong to say that the aims of Greek 'scientists' have been lost sight of entirely. Modern science is indeed in some sense a fulfilment of something begun by the Greeks, one which, though transforming their enterprise almost beyond recognition, has nevertheless preserved what was distinctive and essential to it.

This way of putting the matter is, deliberately, reminiscent of Hegel, for the relation here suggested is as good an example as we are likely to find of Hegel's process of *aufheben*, also discussed in the previous chapter. Hegel, it should be noted, is not himself specially concerned with this particular case, but it will nonetheless serve to illustrate one of the fundamental features of Hegel's philosophy of history. The Aristotelian conception so far discussed employs the idea of a universal 'given', our nature as animals, which is present from the start of the long historical sequence under consideration, and which the order of life favours more and more as history proceeds. However, Hegel thinks that there is something other than our animal nature, which he calls spirit, which is *not* a 'given' at the start of human history, but works itself out, or as he says, realizes itself over time. On the Aristotelian conception each stage of history constitutes a progressive development in so far as it is an improvement on the stage that went before it by enabling human beings to live the sort of life to which they are best suited. Thus each preceding stage is at most a causal contributor to the ability of the succeeding stage to do this. On Hegel's view, by contrast, each age has its own aspirations or ideals, and progress is evidenced by the fact that in succeeding stages these ideals are not merely realized more fully but *aufgehoben*, that is, themselves transformed in a way that changes them, by raising them, while at the same time embodying and hence preserving what is essential to them. The growth of natural science is plausibly one such case. Progress in science has consisted not only, and perhaps not much, in the accumulation of knowledge, but in the development of more and more sophisticated and satisfactory conceptions and standards of scientific knowledge.

On this Hegelian view, we can discern the progressive nature of scientific development only with hindsight, for to repeat his celebrated remark, the owl of Minerva (which is to say, sound judgement), must take its flight at the falling of the dusk, i.e. at the end of a process. We cannot appreciate the enormous advance with which modern science presents us by possessing ourselves of a detailed knowledge of the aims of the early Greeks, because these were formed in a world which could have no idea of what modern scientists are about. That is why a purely 'contextualized' history can never arrive at a wholly adequate understanding of the past. Still less, however, should we try to transcend the limitations of specific periods by fastening upon some idea of the scientific inclinations or yearnings of a universal human nature. There is no such thing. At most what we will find at the outset of science is an inchoate curiosity on the part of human beings, but the history of science is not the story of this curiosity's steady satisfaction. Rather the history of science is the story of its gradual *realization*, a story in which an initial curiosity, which perhaps can be attributed to human nature, is given form and substance, and only thus lent significance. A similar point might be made about the history of language. A natural human impulse to communicate may well lie at the origin of language, but if a modern highly literate language such as English is far richer than the collection of communicative grunts to which, let us suppose, very early peoples were restricted, its greater richness is not to be understood as consisting in a larger vocabulary by means of which constantly present thoughts and desires can be expressed. Rather, the development of language realizes hitherto undreamt of degrees of communication.

If this is correct, and if we assume (as seems reasonable) that scientific advance, still more language use, will have to figure prominently in any belief in progress in the fullest sense, we have reason to conclude that the Hegelian conception of progress is a more promising one than the Aristotelian. However, it appears to have at least one major problem. On the Hegelian scheme of things the point of view with which a progressivist philosophical history must begin is that of the present day. This seems to bring a return of what I called 'epochocentrism', the danger that judgements of progress are prejudiced by the aims and preferences of our own time. If so, the objectivity between ages which the device of the Impartial Observer was intended to secure is jeopardized. Certainly, Hegel is strongly of the opinion that no one can "leap over Rhodes", by which he means that the mind cannot stand outside its own time, and this implies that contemporary minds can work with only modern knowledge and concepts.

What we need to see, however, is that the truth of this contention about the inescapability of historical situatedness in the present does not preclude objective judgement about previous ages. Indeed, since, as I argued in the last chapter, historical judgement is often only possible with hindsight, objective historical understanding actually *requires* a backward perspective. Understanding the development of science, but other cultural forms also, requires an examination of the past in the light of a sound grasp of present conceptions and the ideals implicit within them. What philosophical history will show, if the belief in progress is true, is that the ideals of previous ages have their most satisfactory realization in later ages, so that these later ages are preferable from their own point of view also. And since by definition the present age is the latest, from the point of view of philosophical history it is the best, if, that is to say, progressivism is true.

The impartiality of the Impartial Observer, then, is not eliminated by the Hegelian conception, but revised. We can in fact employ the same formula 4 of the belief in progress, with some little amendment, as that which emerged from the Aristotelian conception, namely:

5. Up to the present time, for any time, there is a later time at which an Impartial Observer would have reason to prefer

to live. This could have been said truly at the majority of past times, but not at every time.[2]

In this formulation, however, the point of view of the IO derives, not from an abstracted human point of view which stands outside any age, but from the vantage point of hindsight, from which alone assessment can be made whether and how one age is truly *aufgehoben* in the next. This is a judgement arrived at by the establishment of historical fact philosophically understood; it is not the a priori assumption of the IO's contemporary concepts and values. Thus, to continue with the example of science, it says that in say, 1750, a philosophical historian of science could in principle articulate the advantages of Newtonian mechanics in such a way as to show how the science of 1750 had successfully superseded the Aristotelian physics of previous periods, while at the same time relating those advantages to the recognized aims and ambitions of the Aristotelian physicist. If a similar explanation can be given both backwards and forwards in time from 1750, even if not at *every* historical juncture, we have succeeded in giving a progressivist account of science along Hegelian lines.

Whether such an account can indeed be given depends crucially, of course, on matters of historical fact as well as philosophical interpretation. For the purposes of exploring the structure of progressivism as one possible shape of the past, however, we need not attempt such an account here. It is enough to have formulated a clear and coherent structure for a progressivist view of science, science being a context in which the belief in progress will strike most people as plausible. The existence of progress in science, however, even if its story can be told adequately, does not show that the shape of the past more generally is progressivist. The point was made earlier that a convincing story of

---

[2] The interpretation of this formula within the Hegelian conception needs one clarification, namely that the minority of times at which this could not have been said would be plateaux rather than dips.

progress in one aspect of history, and even the mere accumulation of several such stories, is not sufficient to sustain a belief in progress overall. It depends on the relative centrality to human culture of the aspects in question.

The social and historical importance of science is an issue of both complexity and dispute. The fact that science is obviously related in some way to productive technology and effective medicine has lent support to the contention of Fukuyama and others that it has played a key role in the historical development of human culture. But it is also true that the most dramatic impact of scientific inquiry in these areas is of relatively recent date; the science of the ancient and mediaeval periods of European history contributed little if anything to increasing economic welfare. It is probable, therefore, that the cultural importance of science has changed over time. Furthermore, even in the modern period some highly important scientific advances, in biology and astronomy for instance, are much less easily tied in with larger social forms. Most importantly, whatever the connections between science and progress in medicine, technology, and prosperity, it seems clear that developments in politics, morality, and possibly religion and art, where any connection with progress in science is much more tenuous, should figure in some way in any general theory of historical progress.

Of course, a believer in progress might try to bring these four dimensions into play, not by connecting them with science, but by attributing progress to them in their own right. To do so, however, raises the prior question whether either of the conceptions of progress developed in this chapter might be made to fit these at all plausibly. Initial plausibility varies between them, as a matter of fact. Given that history reveals the replacement of a world in which slavery was taken for granted by one in which it is universally deplored, the rise of humanitarian concern for the individual, the spread of political equality and the move from oligarchic to democratic forms of government, there is at least an initial plausibility to the claim that history exhibits moral and political progress, whatever doubts may arise on second reflection. But in the case of religion and art most people would not grant even an initial plausibility.

In closing this chapter, therefore, we must shift the focus of the analysis away from the relatively easy cases of science and technology to those of politics, morality, and so on. How does the Impartial Observer accommodate these? Let us stick to the case of morality where, it seems, there is at least an initial plausibility to the progressivist's claims. The Hegelian interpretation of Formula 5 tells us that the IO will be able to give an account which shows how the moral practices and ideals of later periods successfully superseded the practices and ideals of earlier periods, while at the same time being able to relate the preference for later times to the recognized aims and ambitions of those earlier moralities. Hegel's celebrated 'master/slave' dialectic is an abstract example of how this is to be done. In the master/slave relation there is implied a measure of human equality which that relation itself cannot satisfactorily realize. The master requires an element of autonomy on the part of the slave—slaves are not in fact machines—while at the same time requiring also that it be suppressed. For this reason the relationship is inherently unstable, and the modified form which emerges from it is for that reason more adequate.

Now even this brief exposition reveals an important point in the structure of the dialectic. However much the relationship changes, between earlier and later forms there has to be a continuity of deep-seated endeavour. That is to say, the root aim of the two is the same, just as we can see that the root aim of scientists over the ages—to explain and to understand—remains the same, even if their conceptions of what it is to explain and understand undergo deep transformations. But in morality, it has not infrequently been alleged, there is no such continuity. The history of morality includes radical *breaks* between one period and another. Thus, if we suppose that Christian morality was the successor in Europe of Greek and Roman morality, we must acknowledge that it brought with it wholly new virtues and values—humility and chastity[3] for instance—which had no counterparts in the morality it replaced. Similarly with religion. While there may be something to be said for the view that Christianity superseded Judaism in the Hegelian sense (a view to which Hegel did indeed subscribe), it would be much harder to say the same about the relation between Christianity and Roman civic religion. So too with art. The succession of the Baroque by the Classical, then the Romantic, and then the Modern is a widely recognized general historical schema, but not obviously one in which a progressive *aufheben* is at work.

The cases of morality and art may be importantly different, in fact. The history of morality, so it has been alleged, is one in which there are radical breaks, one in which moralities fall into decline and eventual collapse. The mark of this is that as actual ways of life they become unavailable to the inhabitants of later periods, who can view them only as historical curiosities. It is, for instance, impossible for modern men to display the valour and win the honour to which mediaeval knights aspired, and those who stage tournaments nowadays can only properly be regarded as play acting, even if occasionally they take themselves more seriously than this. By contrast, in the case of art earlier forms and ideals remain available in some important ways. Musical genres such as the classical or the romantic, for instance, emerge, develop, and become completed, but they do not wholly disappear into the past. The mark of their completion is the impossibility of continuing to compose in these genres without a sense of copying or pastiche, but contemporary musicians can explore and exploit their own musicality as readily in the Baroque as in the Modern idiom.

---

[3] Some qualification is needed here. Lucretius urges chastity as a virtue.

Between morality and art there is, apparently, this real difference and if it has been accurately described, these aspects of human experience show, in contrast to science and technology, that alternatives to progress as the shape of the past can have greater plausibility—decline and collapse is the story of moralities, and in the case of music the shape is that of completed cycles. To assess the merits of progressivism, consequently, we need to explore the cogency and coherence of these alternative shapes. This will in fact form the subject of the next three chapters, before we will be in a position to return to the consideration of progressivism.

4 Decline

In every age, in every generation perhaps, there are those who believe that the story of the past is one of decline. Often it is right to regard such a belief simply as an expression of pessimism, rather than a serious interpretation of past and present. There appears to be a constant tendency for one generation to think that the next is falling away from higher standards of the right and the good, in religion, morality, education, art and, indeed, in most facets of human existence. Such gloom is aided and abet ted very often by nostalgia, through which the facts are coloured by that curious mixture of pleasure and pain people find in the contemplation of lost youth. Indeed, since it takes a considerable effort to view the world as we knew it when we were young (or even just *younger*), independently of the fact that we were then young, nostalgic appeals to 'the good old days' are common, though perhaps they are less commonly made in all seriousness. But such a category is plainly worthless from the point of view of historical understanding, for history, even the simple history of memory and recall, must distinguish sharply between the nature of the world that was then inhabited and the nature of us who then inhabited it. What history proper wants to know is how things really were, not how they are fondly thought to have been, even if these fond thoughts are the thoughts of those who 'were there'.

Nevertheless, despite the fact that nostalgia easily colours the memory and receding generations almost always lament the past and deplore the present and usually for no better reason than that together they signal their own passing, it is a mistake to conclude that the idea of history's being in decline cannot be taken seriously. To begin with, it is important to guard against what has been called the 'genetic fallacy', the mistake, that is to say, of supposing that an explanation of the *causes* of a belief renders redundant any inquiry into its *grounds*, and hence its truth or falsehood.[1] Similarly, while it may be true that a belief in 'the good old days' or a Golden Age is often generated and sustained by pessimism, nostalgia or wishful thinking, it does not follow that there is no truth in such beliefs. Furthermore, many appeals to a 'Golden Age' are to a period long before the lifetimes of those who make the appeal and cannot therefore easily be dismissed as 'memories of youth coloured by nostalgia'. In fact the idea that the very distant past was a period of perfection when compared with the present is a very old one, exemplified most plainly in the Genesis story according to which there was once a garden of Eden, a paradise in which the normal pains and conflicts of life as we now know it did not exist. Finally, as this example reveals, a belief in decline does not necessarily imply unmitigated pessimism. The Christian theology of salvation includes a belief in 'the Fall', but this is only part of the story; the same theology contains a belief in God's decisive intervention and the prospect of a final redemption in which God "makes all things new".

There are secular counterparts which illustrate the same point. In the eighteenth century, belief in a Golden Age attracted considerable popularity, even amongst philosophers. Rousseau's *Social Contract* begins with the sentence "Man was born free but everywhere he is in chains". Rousseau's self-appointed task, however,

---

[1] This important thought is popularly captured in the familiar saying that the fact that someone is paranoid does not mean 'they' are not out to get him.

is not only to explain the origins of this unfortunate condition, but the way in which political society ameliorates it. Similar 'Golden Age' conceptions regularly animate the thinking of social commentators and cultural theorists, but there are three further important points to observe.

First, it is not necessary to believe that the past was a period of perfection in order to hold that the present is in important ways a period of decline. Second, a belief in the gradual falling away from earlier standards need not imply a belief that the decline is terminal. Many who have believed fervently in cultural decline have not hesitated to advocate remedies for its repair. Third, the belief in decline need not generate regret. Long-term historical decline in some aspects of existence—the decline of magic for instance—might bring only an attitude of welcome on the part of those who hold it.

What these three points show is that the belief in historical decline, which, as we have seen, need not originate in nostalgia, need not be accompanied by pessimism, or even regret, still less despair. And since it is these associated feelings that have given decline theories the poor reputation they generally have, the separation of thesis from associated feeling enables us to look more dispassionately at decline as a strictly historical conception, a contention about the general shape of the past. It is important to be able to do so not least because a good deal of the philosophical and sociological thought most prominent at present invokes just such a shape. In fact sophisticated contemporary versions of historical decline are not far to seek. In the second chapter I mentioned two—those of Richard Rorty and Alasdair MacIntyre. MacIntyre's philosophical history in particular warrants closer scrutiny, but because there is an important distinction to be drawn between contentions about historical decline and closely associated contentions about historical collapse, its more detailed examination will be deferred to the next chapter.

The previous chapter focused chiefly upon science and

technology, which together comprise a plausible basis for progressivism. Less plausible for the belief in progress, each for different reasons, are religion, morality, and art. Each represents an
interesting test case for progressivism in general because the history of all three can rather easily be made to generate distinct
and competing conceptions of the past. In the case of religion
it is decline; the thesis that religion has for a long time been
withering away as a fact of history and (more ambitiously) as a
significant part of historical development, is widespread and pervasive in contemporary thinking, both theological and sociological. In the case of morality the position is more dramatic still,
for as well as the belief that specific moralities and sets of values
have declined, social theorists from Nietzsche to MacIntyre have
postulated the inner collapse of morality itself. The arts, by contrast, though here too theorists of decline can be found, are more
commonly grouped into periods, each with its own cycle of birth,
development and completion. In this chapter I shall first examine the idea of historical decline through the example of religion
and in the next examine the more ambitious thesis of the collapse of morality. The case of art will be reserved for a more general examination of the idea of cycles in Chapter 6.

I

The belief that the passage of time has seen the decline of religion is sometimes labelled the thesis of 'secularization'. This thesis was once very prominent as a theory in professional sociological
inquiry, but 'secularization' is also the name of a general belief
about history, one which has entered quite deeply into contemporary thought about religion and society and whose influence
is to be detected far beyond the confines of academic sociology.
Whereas at one time the thesis was quite general, the widespread
appearance of fundamentalist Islam in non-Western countries

has caused it to be less popularly plausible. Still the thesis even yet commands considerable support if its scope is restricted to Western culture which, very many believe, has undergone a gradual process of secularization over the last two hundred years or more. The idea is that, whereas in the ancient, mediaeval and early modern periods, religion played a large part in the social and intellectual life of Europe, in contemporary modern culture it plays a very small part, and in several places no part at all.

This 'theory' of secularization is not, as we shall see, just a simple description of observed social and historical change. It is in fact part of a rather grander conception of the past in which technological development, increasing prosperity, changing moral standards, and the decline of religion are all interconnected. And, we may observe in illustration of an earlier point, it is a thesis which can be combined with an attitude of either regret or enthusiasm. Religionists, for example, may hold this thesis, and deplore the state of contemporary culture for its irreligion, or secularists may hold it, and welcome the decline in what they regard as oppressive and superstitious systems of belief and practice. Consequently, the thesis of decline in itself can be considered as an historical contention whose evaluative implications are a separate matter.

As an historical contention, however, it is no more simple in its structure than the belief in progress proved to be, and in order to assess it, we have first to understand this structure. 'Secularization' shares two important features with the belief in progress. Although its origins are further back, it first finds its most explicit formulation in the nineteenth century, and this formulation, moreover, owes a good deal to Hegel. Several features of Hegel's philosophy of history have already been discussed at some length. Here we need only emphasize that part of the final culmination of history, on Hegel's view, is the rationalization of Christianity into philosophy. Philosophy, by his account, gives a properly rational form to the truths that are embodied but obscured within the

Christian religion. In so saying, Hegel did not himself mean to imply that philosophy eliminates Christianity, but it was a conclusion that subsequent theorists rapidly drew. Ludwig Feuerbach, one of Hegel's immediate successors, is a good example. His influential work, *The Essence of Christianity*, is an attempt to demystify the language of religion, and hence replace it, by systematic reinterpretation into humanistic terms. Thus divine attributes, in the hands of Feuerbach, become idealizations of human aspirations and capacities.

More striking still is the elimination of religion in the writings of Karl Marx, where Feuerbach's humanism is rejected in favour (as Marx believed) of a more thoroughgoing and consistent materialist interpretation of Hegel's general historical framework. Marx saw technological advance under capitalism, with its enormous productive capacity, as the source of humankind's liberation from drudgery. This liberation, however, would be realized only when the economic and social order which had made it possible—capitalism—was radically restructured. Within the Marxian picture the progressive development of history renders religion redundant not in theoretical but in practical terms. Religion, for Marx, is an opiate of the people, an image that has quite often been misunderstood. To declare religion an opiate is to regard it as a painkiller, and as such it can play an important role in numbing the miseries to which human beings are prey. Religion directs our attention away from this world to another, one "without pain or grief but life eternal", and the belief in such a world serves, somewhat paradoxically, to sustain us in the unremitting miseries of this one. But once the technological means of actually ameliorating the hardships of human existence are at hand, the comforting illusions of religion will be abandoned, not because they are discovered to be false, but because they are no longer needed. Technology, we might say, renders prayer redundant, and as a postcapitalist society emerges, religion, no less than the state, will wither away.

Auguste Comte, another nineteenth-century philosopher of history on the grand scale whose views have already been mentioned briefly, is also a theorist of secularization. Comte divides the past into stages. The first of these is the theological, when the natural world was believed to be full of animating spirits. The theological stage gave way to the metaphysical, at which point men sought rationalistic explanations. In its turn this has been replaced by the scientific age, or in Comte's terminology, the 'positive' age, when we demand the sort of natural explanations and empirical evidence that are found in physical science. According to this view of the past, it is not just that technology, through its greater successes, causes religion to lose its appeal. Rather, the level of understanding which may properly be called theological is historically primitive, and though it is certainly a necessary stage in the course of mankind's development, it is of no value in later phases. Over time, so to speak, the human mind marches on and leaves its religious impulses behind.

Feuerbach, Marx, and Comte are Hegelians, not in the sense that they are expositors, still less disciples, of Hegel's philosophical views, but because they share his conception of history as a story of the progressive development of human culture, the principles of which can be uncovered by investigation. And since the decline of religion is part of their account, it is clear that decline and progress are not necessarily opposed conceptions of the shape of the past—the decline of some aspect of culture, religion in this case, can be accommodated within a more general belief in progress overall. Nevertheless, their treatment of religion can be isolated as an instance which will serve the investigation of the nature of belief in historical decline. As such it has two important features. First, the decline of religion is structural. That is to say, it is a phase through which human beings have passed and which they have outgrown because of general connections which hold between different aspects of culture. Second, the decline in religion is a matter of recordable, and recorded, fact.

Indeed all three of these theorists, it seems to me, regarded the decline of religion as evident, a belief that is still widely shared.

These two features are clearly crucial, and though as we shall see, they are interrelated, they coincide with a very broad distinction between the philosophical and the historical. Empirical history records a steady decline in religion, and an adequate philosophical understanding of the development of the human mind will show why this is only to be expected. But if, in examining the thesis, our principal concern is with the second question, we must not take the common assumption of recorded secularization for granted, but ask whether the history of religion is indeed one of decline, and how the evidence might be marshalled in answering this question.

II

So far I have spoken of 'religion'. But in fact secularization is really a thesis about Christianity. It has seemed and still seems evident to many that the Christian religion is in terminal decline. The evidence in favour of this falls broadly into two kinds. First there is evidence about the social extent of religious observance, and second, evidence about the role of religious ideas in intellectual life. Let us consider these in turn.

It is a commonplace that across the whole of Western Europe Christian observance shows a steady diminution over some considerable period of time. It has been estimated that in 1985 within the countries of Western Europe 86 per cent of people had no connection of any kind with organized religion, and for many of the remaining 14 per cent any connection is extremely tenuous. In short, at the end of the twentieth century the vast majority of modern West Europeans know nothing and care less about organized Christianity. To this statistic about mass participation we may add many others. These show a steep decline in the number of vocations to priesthoods and ministries, and near collapse in vocations to religious orders. Thousands of church buildings all over Europe are empty and crumbling. Others have been converted to museums or commercial stores, depending upon their architectural merits. In brief, if the facts are allowed to speak for themselves, the present parlous state of organized religion is indisputable.

Such at any rate is the received wisdom, but like so many commonplaces, what is here presented as indisputable is in fact highly disputable. Much of this 'evidence' is based upon survey techniques whose methodology is questionable and whose results do not altogether sustain the inferences that are drawn from them. Statistics, it cannot be said often enough, are as valuable as the cogency of their interpretation. However, despite any such shortcomings, there is enough support for the contention that religious observance is a small part of contemporary culture to allow us to suppose that evidence to this effect could indeed be mustered. Even so, it is possible to acknowledge the existence, or at least possibility, of such evidence and still contest the thesis that Christianity is in evident decline. We need not dispute the truth or significance of statistical claims, for example, in order to make the logical point that by themselves they cannot confirm the thesis of secularization. To begin with, for the thesis to hold good, the present state of religion must contrast with a previous, much stronger state. In other words, we can infer from the statistics that religious observance is in decline only if we have good evidence that the relevant figures would have been much higher in the past. Most people assume that such evidence exists. They suppose that there is a sharp contrast between the extent of church-going in contemporary Britain, for instance, and church-going in the Victorian period. However, it is far from clear that this supposition could be borne out by evidence. Not least this is because comparable statistics for Victorian Britain do not exist, and other evidence suggests that did they do so, they would be less clear cut. Here, for instance, is Engels' description of religion among the English working classes, which is to say the large majority of the population, in 1844: "[A]mong the masses there prevails almost universally a total indifference to religion, or at the utmost some trace of deism too undeveloped to amount to more than mere words or a vague dread of the words 'infidel', 'atheist' etc." (*State of the Working Class in England in 1844*, p. ix).

Engels, in keeping with the Hegelian framework of thought which he shares with Marx, confidently expected further decline. This has not obviously occurred, and the picture among lower-income groups now is in many respects very much what it was then. In fact, though it is relatively easy to show that attendance in a specific denomination in a given geographical area has declined very seriously within a specific period—Methodism in the North of England since World War I, for instance, or Roman Catholicism in the Netherlands since the Second Vatican Council—it is very hard to substantiate empirically any more general claim even about one country. Consequently, to move from specific cases to a more general thesis about religious observance across Europe since the Enlightenment or the French Revolution is to move very far beyond what any available evidence could warrant. Still less do detailed statistics about limited times and places tell us anything about the relation between Christian belief and contemporary Western culture.

These doubts about adequate evidence for the thesis of secularization are important. But it ought to be observed that providing an empirical basis in established fact for *any* social thesis is always a complex matter, and not one that can be settled without prolonged and detailed investigation, which it may not always be possible to conduct satisfactorily. It would be a weak argument, consequently, which relied for its rejection entirely upon the uncertainty of empirical evidence. Perhaps 'best estimate' is the most we can do, and if so, there seems considerable plausibility in the thesis that the extent and role of religion in contemporary Western society is not what it was.

However, we must set alongside its plausibility some other striking facts. There is a serious danger that the experience of Europe, localized both in time and space, is used to present a distorted picture of the whole. Even if the sort of evidence about contemporary and past religious observance that is normally presented could be made to show a widespread and steady decline across Western Europe, it is only part of a larger picture. There is no similar decline in the United States, where church attendance remains at a very high level. In Eastern Europe, following the collapse of communist regimes, interest in the Christian religion rose dramatically. In many Third World countries the number of Christians is growing. (In view of the striking fact that across the world adherence to Islam seems to be gathering strength, it is important to recall that we are here restricting the thesis of secularization to Christianity.)

These well-known and equally incontestable facts provide a useful check to any uncritical acceptance of the secularization thesis, but they fall very far short of a refutation of it. There are a number of plausible explanations that could make the facts and the thesis compatible. For instance, it might be said that the sort of popular Christianity we find in the southern United States is not evidence that religion can persist under conditions of intellectual progress, precisely because southern Baptism and the like is a reaction against intellectually induced liberalism, a sort of rear-guard action against the inevitability of secularization. Contemporary conservative religionists might thus be said to fit Marx's description of the feudalists of his own day: "[H]alf lamentation, half lampoon; half echo of the past, half menace of the future; at times . . . striking . . . to the very heart's core; but always ludicrous in its effect, through total incapacity to comprehend the march of modern history" (*Communist Manifesto*, p. 106).

Alternatively it might be argued, as Alasdair MacIntyre once argued in *Secularization and Moral Change*, American religion has been itself secularized. In other words, the emergence and development of American churches has been so deeply influenced by secular trends, that they cannot properly be taken to represent a survival of *religion*. Similarly, proponents of the secularization thesis could discount the recent experience of Eastern Europe, on the ground that long years of persecution have forged an association between religion and social and personal freedom so close that what is attractive to contemporary East Europeans is not the religion itself so much as the aspiration to freedom it represents. Finally, the third body of evidence alluded to— evidence from Third World countries—is by and large evidence from a pre-industrialized world, and the greater extent of religion under such conditions, it can be argued, is just what the thesis of secularization would lead one to expect; religion persists where technological and industrial development has not yet taken a hold, or not yet taken sufficient hold.

In these various ways, evidence which appears to count against the thesis can be explained away. Nor should these explanations be dismissed as mere face-saving ploys. Still, what the necessity of appealing to them shows is that a, perhaps unavoidable, move has been made from the first sort of evidence—the social extent of religious observance—to the second, that is, evidence about the role of religious ideas in intellectual and cultural life. The auxiliary explanations just canvassed not only suppose that the real test of the thesis must reside in more than empirical survey of the state of religious practice. It must also satisfactorily relate such facts to the general cultural context in which they hold. It is not the mere presence or extent of religion which matters, but its role in social and intellectual life. And, we might add, they further suppose Western Europe to be the cradle of scientific and technological advance, and hence the truest conditions under which the continuing relevance of religion is put to the test.

In advancing such explanations there is of course a danger of circularity. It is easy to claim that once Eastern Europe advances to the same stage of prosperity and freedom as Western Europe, the attractions of religion will fade there too. But if the argument in favour of this claim is that such has been the course of Western European history, then the whole thesis is circular. To avoid this circularity we need another ground upon which to base the thesis, one which will allow us to assess the respective merits of the various pieces of evidence.

III

The appeal to contemporary cultural context which the thesis of secularization must make is more ambitious than it might appear. If the thesis is to preserve its character as a claim about the general shape of the past, it needs to do more than record a periodic shift in cultural trends. It is not enough, even if true, that contemporary Western culture invokes religious ideas less than it did in some earlier periods. It must also be shown that this movement is in some way ineluctable. One familiar stratagem by which this further move is made, or at least implied, is in terms of appeal to a mentality, namely that of the modern mind. The idea is that the developing intellectual structures which gave rise to modern science and technology, with their resultant prosperity, have created a mentality which can no longer accept the magical and supernatural elements that are an essential part of religion. It is against this background that the facts of religious observance are to be ordered and understood, for by so locating it, evidence of continuing attachment to religion can indeed be explained as mere attachment to residual intellectual habits. The proof that religion is in decline will thus lie ultimately, not with statistical evidence, but with evidence of the increasing irrelevance of religious and theological ideas for contemporary intellectual inquiry.

On the face of it, evidence of this sort too seems no less abundant. Modern medicine relies upon tablets prescribed by biochemistry and pharmacology rather than upon religious charms and incantations, or the prescribed prayers of the church, and though people do still pray for good health on the part of themselves, their friends and family, the greater 'faith' of most patients, Christian and non-Christian, is revealed by their behaviour to be in the techniques of the physician and the surgeon. Similarly, natural science no longer employs supernatural agency in its explanations—the new physics has replaced Aquinas's cosmological argument, and Darwin has replaced divine design. Again, history is generally preferred to hagiography, and modern historians do not, because they cannot, take the stories of biblical miracles very seriously. The modern world, we might say, has been emptied of devils and angels, along with fairies and goblins, and no one nowadays believes that water can miraculously turn into wine.

It is worth noting that this account of modernity and 'the modern mind' however plausible initially, is not much less selective of the facts than the more straightforwardly empirical evidence which it was called upon to support. To begin with, the attitudes here cited as 'modern' have precursors more ancient than most who speak in this way generally suppose. Although, to take just one example, historical criticism of the Bible of the sort which discounts the miraculous is commonly thought to be a product of the nineteenth century, we can find John Bunyan two hundred years before arguing ferociously against the Ranters for holding just this sort of view (Hill, chap. 7). Conversely, what contemporaneously existing people, who are familiar with and make extensive use of the latest technology, are prepared to believe is surprisingly varied. Modern medicine is certainly dominant, but alternative forms of remedy are still common and faith healers abound. Astrology is certainly not respectable among scientists, but modern politicians are known to have consulted the stars. Talk of devils and angels is not widespread, though perhaps it never was, but there are plenty of witches' covens in Western Europe, and the Roman Catholic Church, in which there have been many canonizations in recent years, has no difficulty in

finding witnesses to the necessary miracles. Even amongst intellectuals, belief in the supernatural cannot be said to be dead.
There are respected physicists who believe in the traditional God
of theism, and prominent biologists who think that there is
evidence of design in nature, even some who think that special
creation is a better explanation than natural selection.

Of course, all these phenomena can in their turn be explained
as residual superstitions, though to make this move is to reveal
once again how the thesis of secularization must be selective of
the facts about modern life, regarding some as truly revelatory
of the modern mind, and others as wholly discountable. But, as
with the statistical findings, this selectivity opens up the danger
of circularity. In order to sustain the thesis in the face of apparently contrary empirical facts, appeal was made to the development of 'the modern mind', a mentality fashioned by its critical,
scientific, and naturalistic character. It now seems that in order
to declare this mentality 'modern' we must ignore many aspects
of what modern people actually believe. We must dismiss all those
beliefs, however widely held, which do not accord with our pre-
conception of what can and cannot constitute 'the modern mind'.
This begs the question, however, for if by 'the modern mind' we
mean 'ways in which contemporaneously existing people think',
then 'the modern mind' contains a good measure of belief in the
supernatural and the magical

In short, the mentality which is here declared modern has no
special claim to that title if we construe the phrase 'the modern
mind' to be descriptive of what people living at this time actually believe. It follows that the appeal to such a mentality can be
made to work in defence of the secularization thesis only if it is
given a more normative interpretation, one in which 'the modern mind' ceases to be a relatively plain empirical description
and becomes instead a standard by which the beliefs of existing
people are to be assessed. The necessity of such a move is in fact
in keeping with the way in which ideas of being modern and up

to date are commonly used—in a boring sense everything existing at present is 'up to date', but since the old fashioned can exist
at the present, the phrase 'up to date' must be given a normative interpretation.

So too with 'the modern mind', which is not so much a conception of how people do as a matter of fact think, but how,
given contemporary standards of rationality, they ought to think.
This needs to be both an intellectual and an historical 'ought'—
the failure to take a scientific approach to medicine is a fault *now*,
but it was not in times past. It is this historically formed rationality which gives history a measure of the necessary. Religious
beliefs were once common among human beings, but the development of a distinctive mentality—the modern, scientific mind—
prevents them from becoming common again. The picture at
work here is very much that of Comte's philosophy of history.
There is a sort of ratchet development in the history of human
thought. Each phase in the development has arisen out of a
former phase to which it is impossible to return.

Whatever the nature of this impossibility, however, it cannot
be a straightforwardly historical or sociological one. Granted that
there are at least some people, not noticeably dissociated from
the world of science and technology, who persist with magical
and supernatural views, it is plainly possible that such people
should as a matter of fact come to form the majority. Contemporary Western education works against it, certainly, but this is also
another contingent fact. If astrology, cures by incantation, and
belief in miraculous events were inculcated in our schools with
the same seriousness that the lessons of natural science and political history are, they might easily produce a condition in which
belief in magic and supernatural agencies was once more widespread
and respected. And this possibility is enough to show that there
is in fact nothing in the inevitability of secularization which could
give us reason to believe it to be finally established or complete.

Beliefs of the Comtean sort about the decline of religion often rest upon the idea that 'the modern mind' has put away childish things and can no more return to a mentality in which religion and magic feature, than the adult can return to childhood. Indeed, in giving a shape to the past people have not infrequently used the idea that the distant past is the childhood of humanity. But of course at best this is just an analogy. Humankind does not have a childhood, adulthood, and so on, in the way that an individual human being does, and the ease with which references of this sort are made does not show the contrary. It is best therefore to regard 'the modern mind' as primarily an intellectual norm, which tells us not so much what sort of beliefs are as a matter of fact, or historically must be, held in industrial and postindustrial society, but what sort of beliefs ought to be held.

This further refinement of the thesis requires that the evaluative ambivalence over the decline of religion and the rise of the modern mind must now be resolved. Faced with the socio/historical thesis that religion is in terminal decline, we are free either to welcome or deplore this fact. But in invoking 'the modern mind' as a norm, we move from the claim that religious decline is inevitable, to the claim that it is desirable. It is thus a move from a belief in secularization to a belief in secularism, and because of this invocation of norms, a move to philosophical history proper as it was described in Chapter 2.

IV

Those who believe in secularism need not consider themselves satisfactorily refuted by the arguments so far advanced. It is common to hear the possibility of widespread religious revival accepted (the growth of Islamic fundamentalism makes this possibility something of a reality), but accepted as some sort of return to 'the Dark Ages'. Secularists need not suppose that history is complete and that the modern age is its perfect, irreversible, fulfilment, but they are sure to think that certain changes in social beliefs and practices would be retrograde. If it did come about that school lessons in magic and witchcraft were given with the same cultural seriousness as are lessons in science and history, this would have to be regarded by modernists, not merely as a different period of history with its own standards, but as a significant loss in terms of real understanding. To think in this way is to acknowledge a distinction between enlightened and unenlightened minds, and to regard the modern mind as the more enlightened.

Two points are specially worth noting here. First, by a somewhat curious route, a thesis about decline as a shape of the past has become allied with a belief in progress. This is not really surprising. Progressive developments of even the simplest type will necessarily contain aspects of decline. Thus, the advent of electric lighting brought with it the decline of the gas mantle. Progress and decline, then, are not alternative or incompatible *shapes* which we may give to history. They become alternatives only when they are allied to competing evaluations. The decline in religion may be deplored by religionists, but it can be seen as a progressive development once it has been fitted into a scheme in which the decline of religion becomes an aspect of modernity. As such however it still provides us with a useful, familiar and plausible example which will serve to illuminate how any conception of historical decline must be structured. And an essential part of this structure is the evaluative component just uncovered.

Second, although this evaluative element has been identified as a belief in enlightenment, the distinction between enlightenment and unenlightenment can be employed independently of a conception of history. In fact there is a real question as to whether there is anything peculiarly modern about enlightenment, or whether most of history is not an exchange between enlightenment and unenlightenment. That is to say, doubts may be raised about the historical dimension which is usually given to this important distinction. It is not a modernist, after all, but Barrabas in Marlowe's *Jew of Malta* who says "I count religion but a toy, and hold there is no sin but ignorance".

However, we may leave this second doubt aside because once we distinguish between the sociological claims of secularization and the evaluative claims of secularism, the central question for both historical and non-historical versions is whether religion lies on the side of enlightenment or unenlightenment.

Secularism holds that the decline of religion is desirable because religion is a facet of the unenlightened mind. How might this contention be established? Evidence of a sort is not hard to assemble. First, we need only look at the history of religion, and the history of Christianity especially perhaps, to see that it has stimulated some of the most undesirable acts and institutions in human history —the ostracism of the Jews over centuries, the Inquisition, the wars and persecutions of the Reformation period, the destructive effects of Christian teaching on sex, the frightening of children with thoughts of hell. As Lucretius says *"Tantum religio potuit suadere malorum"*—such evil deeds could religion prompt—and the list of these deeds is almost endless. Furthermore, according to the secularists, the sort of intolerance, enmity, and strife which only religion can generate is to be found still wherever religious enthusiasm persists, whether in Iran or Northern Ireland.

Not only has Christianity prompted these phenomena, it has constantly provided apologists for those opposed to progressive development. Christian preachers were not in short supply who would speak in opposition to vaccination against smallpox, the abolition of slavery, the development of social welfare, or the introduction of family planning. All these major improvements in the lot of mankind found large numbers of Christian opponents.

A second point in favour of the view that the religious mind is essentially unenlightened is the constant tendency of Christianity (as also Islam) throughout its history, in the form both of ecclesiastical institutions and individual minds, to stifle intellectual criticism in the name of and for the sake of groundless dogma, to demand a faith that 'does not question how'. In its Roman Catholic version the individual intellect must give way to the infallible dictates of the Pope in Council; in its Protestant version, reason must yield to faith; since the Gospel cannot be proved, it can only be preached, or so the highly celebrated theologian Karl Barth was wont to contend. The anti-intellectualism inherent in religion is perhaps the strongest evidence of its opposition to enlightenment, and to many people it demonstrates a deep antithesis between religious belief and the fundamental requirements of a modern education. For the aim of education as we generally understand it is the inculcation of a spirit of critical questioning on the one hand, and on the other the provision of means by which self-generated answers may be discovered. Religion, by contrast, seems to require subscription to dogma and submission to religious authorities whether ecclesiastical or scriptural. In short, the history of Christianity, in common with many other religions, shows it to be a constant force against enlightenment, and hence against the scientific, technical, economic, and psychological advances that come with enlightenment.

There are many who will sympathize with this robustly negative characterization of religion, especially Western monotheistic religion. Nevertheless, there is a substantial measure of selectivity in the picture here presented. If the history of Christianity contains anti-intellectual elements, which it certainly does, it also includes the creation of universities and other places of education and learning. Indeed, it has not infrequently been argued with considerable plausibility that the development of modern science and critical history has its intellectual origins in the Christian religion.[2] Christians, too, were a major influence on the abolition of the slave trade, the improvement of social conditions,

---

[2] See for instance Michael B. Foster, 'The Christian Doctrine of Creation and the Rise of Modern Natural Science', *Mind*, 43 (1934).

and the extension of equality. The plain consideration of historical fact will not produce a clear case for either the prosecution or defence.

This only shows, however, that the simple instantiation of fact is insufficient to settle the issue. Despite much evidence that could be assembled to the contrary, a great deal of contemporary thought does accept that there is truth in the claim that traditional religion is unsuited to modernity because of its being broadly opposed to the enlightenment ideals which characterize the modern world. This opposition is not to be revealed by a simple adding up of historical episodes, but by the interpretation of history in terms of unifying conceptions, of which 'the modern mind' is the most central. Importantly, the belief in an inherent tension between religion and enlightenment is not simply the view of anti-religious secular humanists. It is shared by both neo-conservative and modernist Christians, who have defined their respective self-conceptions in terms of it and something useful may be learned by considering these pro-religious views as well.

Neo-conservative theology, of the sort espoused by Barth for instance, is fundamentally opposed to the rationalism of the Enlightenment. Under the influence of one interpretation of St Paul, but also of the Lutheran pietist tradition as exemplified by Kierkegaard, reformed theology of this kind not only holds that faith requires neither proof nor evidence, but positively demands their absence. In line with Barth's general thinking, it eschews all attempts at natural theology in preference to uncontaminated revelation. The refinements which will be found in Barth's very extensive theological writings are important, but the general thrust of his view is common to a more popular conservatism in religion, which regards liberal, rationalistic enlightenment as corrosive of faith, and views the attempt to supply 'reasons' for religious belief as the mark of a 'corrupt generation that seeks a sign' (Luke 11: 29). At its extreme, one realized in some present day Southern Baptist seminaries, all free, rational inquiry is to be avoided, because of its potential conflict with revealed theology which is the sole guide to the truths necessary for salvation. Such an attitude to free thinking is difficult to sustain in practice in the modern world because the application of certain sorts of reasoning plays such an important part in social life; the most fundamentalist preachers use the most modern telecommunications systems. Some sects—the Amish for instance—do succeed in applying it to larger areas of life than others, though here too there are substantial incursions from contemporary practice in economics and technology. But what lies behind all these various conservative positions, is a belief that modernity is the enemy of Christian religion, and must therefore be resisted.

By contrast, what used to be known as radical theology responds by trying to *accommodate* the modern mind, also in the belief that modernity and religion as it has hitherto been conceived do not mix. The emergence of a 'modernist' apologetic for Christian theology was closely connected in Britain with the publication in 1963 of John Robinson's famous book *Honest to God*. Several commentators have pointed out, however, that apologetic of this sort can be traced back at least to Friedrich Schleiermacher, widely regarded as the founder of modern theology. As the title of his *On Religion: Speeches to its Cultured Despisers* suggests, Schleiermacher aimed to convince those who were imbued with the intellectual habits of the Enlightenment that there was a version of Christianity which would stand up to their criticisms. Schleiermacher's efforts were not in fact novel. The seventeenth-century Digger Gerrard Winstanley argued in a similar vein and for similar reasons that in understanding the Gospels, mystery is more important than history and that the Christ within us is more important than the Christ who died at Jerusalem. Still, the influence of this idea of a modern mind is very evident in other branches of Christian thought, in Rudolf Bultman's desire to 'demythologize' the Scriptures, for instance, and Dietrich Bonhoeffer's attempts to formulate a 'religionless Christianity'.

The aspiration is plain enough in all of them; we strip the Christian religion of mythological and supernatural elements in terms of which the thought of the ancient world was formed, and attempt to uncover a kernel which will not be foolishness to modern-day, scientifically educated, Gentiles (see 1 Corinthians 1: 23). To a considerable extent modernist Christian thought has required rewriting orthodox theology, with the dual aim of preserving the heart of the Gospel and presenting it in a version that would be acceptable to 'modern man'. These two aims can obviously come into conflict; if the mark of a 'relevant' Gospel is taken to be what 'modern man' finds acceptable, there can be no guarantee that this will coincide in any respect with what first-century Palestine man thought worth proclaiming, and the 'revised' version may have little claim to be a version of Christianity at all. This is the belief at work in much of the criticism of modern theology, but more to the purpose here are the assumptions behind it, first that there is such a thing as the modern, enlightened mind to which the Gospel may or may not be made relevant, and secondly that Schleiermacher and his successors know what it is. If there is no such thing, or if we cannot be sure of its nature, all such attempts are misconceived.

V

The idea of the modern mind, indeed of 'modernity' (though this is a term with slightly wider application) is thus essential to both secularism and two of the religious reactions it has prompted. It is an idea inextricably linked with a conception of history such as we find in Comte, and if this conception cannot be defended, the whole idea of modernity is without foundation. Here, however, we are concerned only with the limited idea that, if there is a modern enlightened mind, it has no place for religion.

The supposition of secularism, radical theology, and for that matter religious neo-conservatism, is that modern thought has no place for the mythological or the supernatural. To ask whether this is true, we need to be clear what we mean by religion. In so doing there are two attendant dangers. First, we may make too many concessions to the idea of modernity and arrive at a conception of religion which has effectively emptied it of supernatural content. For instance, those theologians who, following Schleiermacher's lead, have successfully persuaded 'cultured despisers' to take religion seriously by arguing that God is "whatever is of ultimate concern"[3] have won a hollow victory, since they have made the object of worship dependent on the worshipper rather than the worshipper dependent on the object of worship. They have thus robbed it of any independent reality (an implication which the most radical forms of theological 'antirealism' expressly endorse, naturally[4]). If the *ultimate* nature of these concerns is a function of the depth of human attachment to them, and if this attachment is an aspect of the natural religiosity of human beings, then the supernatural has been 'explained' by effectively denying its existence.

Second, if we define religion in the terms of the ancient, largely prehistoric world, as secularists tend to do, we will have effectively settled the question in advance. Besides religion, there is superstition and magic. Both of these continue to attract believers and practitioners, but there is good reason to hold that these are indeed incompatible with scientific methods of understanding, just as there is reason to think that hagiography cannot sit alongside history proper. To insist on identifying religion with magic, superstition, and hagiography, therefore, is also to settle the question in advance.

So, let us define religion as a belief in the supernatural. By 'supernatural' we must mean not something which simply eschews investigation and explanation by naturalistic, positivistic methods,

---

[3] Tillich, for instance.

[4] For example, Don Cupitt, *Taking Leave of God*.

as the occult does, but something which continues to resist it. The supernatural, properly so called, is anything whose working cannot be formulated and explained by natural laws, and which cannot be subsumed in the chain of material cause and effect. On this account supernatural phenomena will be phenomena that cannot be naturalized, phenomena that we cannot properly conceive of being given naturalistic explanation.

What are these phenomena? The candidates that most immediately spring to mind tend to be ghosts, poltergeists, unexplained cures, voices from the grave, and the like. It is not these, however, that are important, for they can be relegated to the realms of the magical and occult, as indeed orthodox religion has traditionally relegated them.[5] More interesting are the phenomena of mind and soul—knowledge, will, rationality, moral sense, and so on. Whether these might be given wholly natural explanations is a more contentious matter than might be supposed. Since dualistic philosophies of mind and knowledge are broadly out of favour, the general project of naturalization has a large following in contemporary philosophy and attempts are regularly made to offer a naturalized epistemology,[6] or philosophy of mind,[7] or even rationality.[8] Many philosophers would claim that, even if all attempts to date have failed, as they are generally agreed to have done, there are no phenomena of which we cannot properly hope to give a naturalized account. If so, the definition of supernatural with which we are working here, even if it does allow us to distinguish the truly supernatural from the merely unexplained, captures nothing real.

However, anything plausibly called 'the modern mind' subscribes, arguably, to at least one such phenomenon, namely the

---

[5] On this see Keith Thomas, *Religion and the Decline of Magic*.

[6] For example Fred I. Dretske, *Knowledge and the Flow of Information*.

[7] For example Jerry Fodor, *The Language of Thought*.

[8] For example Alan Gibbard, *Wise Choices, Apt Feelings*.

advancement of naturalistic science itself. According to the conception of history we have been considering, scientific and technological advance are central marks of the modern world, and supply an essential part of the driving force behind modernity. The most plausible version of the thesis that religion has declined, we have seen, is not the mere observation of a reduction in the extent of religious practice, because some account must also be given of the notable continuation of religious practices in many places. Rather, we need an account of historical change which will give us reason to regard the perpetuation of such practices, where this occurs, as 'residual', and this requires that we be able to find an incompatibility between these practices and the heart of contemporary culture. Hence the thesis that the success of the natural sciences and their technological application has rendered any serious appeal to the supernatural redundant. But why are the great benefits of technological innovation, modern education, the development of the welfare state, and so on, to be valued? The answer is, presumably, that this way lies the amelioration, and possibly perfection of the human condition—the end of ignorance, illness, and poverty. In short, the application of human will and intelligence through the methods of scientific enlightenment can eventually, in the words of the psalmist, bring us out of the miry clay and set our feet upon a rock. What this belief supposes is that human will and intelligence are not themselves, or not altogether, subject to the natural condition out of which we are to be raised. Faith in human enlightenment is a diluted form of the belief in human perfectibility, and this implies that though the nature of plants and other animals may be 'given', the nature of human beings is not, or not wholly, and that it is possible to rise above nature, even our own nature, in order to perfect it. This 'rising above' may be manifested in relatively simple ways (body building for instance), or more sophisticated ways (mechanized agriculture might be an example), but in either case, will and intelligence are not bounded by natural processes.

Furthermore, their exercise rests upon the hope of something better and a faith in our capacity to realize it.

Here however we encounter a belief in the *super*natural, something immanent in nature but which also transcends nature, whose activity is not bound by the inexorable working of natural law but may progress beyond it through innovation, creation, and self-creation. These terms themselves, though employed here accurately enough, use language which reveals the fundamentally religious character of the belief—hope, faith, transcendence, immanence, creation—all of them traditional theological terms. Their use in this context, it should be stressed, is not intended to deride the modernist's belief in scientific advance. On the contrary, it is an important part of the argument with which this chapter is concerned that the belief in advances of this kind is fundamental to contemporary human self-understanding. What the appositeness of the language shows, however, is that far from belief in the supernatural being antithetical to the modern mind, it is essential to it.

There is a strong temptation to suppose that this conclusion depends upon some sleight of hand in the definition of the supernatural, but it is hard to find reasons in support of such a supposition. It is clear that if we are not to beg the question, the supernatural must not be encumbered with notions that are indeed outmoded by science, as magic is perhaps. Any adequate definition, therefore, must deliberately exclude elements commonly associated with it. However, if the conflict with modern science under discussion is a real one, we can hardly do better than to define the supernatural as that which modern naturalistic science cannot accommodate. So, the definition of the supernatural employed here seems as plausible as any that would be adequate to the purpose. A further doubt about it might arise from the fact that the supernatural agency which turns out to be indispensable for modernity is the human mind itself and not the God of traditional theism, and this might be thought to have so emptied the conception of the supernatural that it becomes in effect a modernistic notion. But nothing said about the eliminability of the supernatural from modern thought excludes the possibility, or for that matter the necessity, that an adequate understanding of human agency should eventually subsume it in a hierarchy of supernatural powers and relations, one which turns out to require the reintroduction of an omnipotent and eternal agent.

Interesting though this conclusion may be, the purpose of this chapter is not to argue directly about the religiosity of modern thought, but to use the example of religion to examine the idea of historical decline. On this issue the following lessons can be learned. First, in illustration of the central contention of Chapter 2 we have seen that the familiar thesis of secularization, which invokes the idea of decline, inevitably passes beyond anything that could be considered mere historical description and employs evaluative, interpretative conceptions—of modernity, advance, superstition, and religion. Second, the last chapter ended with the question whether the conception of historical progress, which most plausibly applies to science and technology, could be extended to other aspects of human experience. What this chapter has shown through the consideration of religion, is that these other aspects, or some of them, can be accommodated into a general progressivism indirectly as well as directly. Thus, claims of decline need not be incompatible with the claim of historical progress, since the decline in question may be an integral part of a larger progressivist picture. Finally, the discussion of the supernatural in modern thought illustrates a further interesting possibility, that an aspect of experience which appears to have declined may in fact have undergone a transformation. Religious conceptions, no less than those of science, may alter, and by sloughing off associated conceptions such as those of magic and superstition, themselves be understood to have been the subject of progressive transformation.

In short, the argument of this chapter has not only illustrated the general claims advanced earlier about philosophical history, but shown that the progressivist interpretation of the past cannot be satisfactorily refuted by the invocation of decline, and may even be strengthened where the decline in question is the plausible case of religion. The reason for this is the relative ease with which, in two ways, decline may be accommodated by the progressive picture. What may be less easy to accommodate is any claim about a radical break between past and present, such as is represented by the dramatic collapse of some marked feature of historical human experience, and it is this possibility that forms the subject-matter of the next chapter.

5 Collapse

THE point we have reached is this: giving a shape to the past is
an exercise in philosophical history and this requires not only
appeal to historical fact, but the employment of normative conceptions in terms of which the facts are to be organized and interpreted. It is chiefly in the exploration of the structure of these
conceptions that philosophical analysis and argument is required.

One such conception is progress, and the idea that the past is
best understood as a story of human progress has had many advo-
cates, as well as detractors. To make sense of it we need to elaborate a transhistorical point of view that will allow the making
of judgements with respect to the relative merits of different
periods, while at the same time avoiding the apriorism which results from the illicit assumption of the values or cultural presuppositions of just one period. In addition, we need to accommodate
the advantages of hindsight for historical understanding. All three
of these requirements can be met in a modified Hegelian philosophy of history, according to which the vantage point of the
present can justifiably be invoked if we can explain the past as a
process of both continuity and change in which the aims and
values of preceding generations are preserved but transformed
to ever greater degrees of refinement and differentiation. The
growth of science and technology can be explained in this way,
and since the historical development of science and technology
provides one of the most plausible candidates for progress, the
Hegelian conception can be given considerable credence. However,
the emergence of successful science is only one aspect of human

history, and before endorsing any more general version of progressivism, we need to inquire whether other features of human experience lend themselves to the same interpretation. The candidates that put the issue most clearly to the test are religion, morality, and art, the first because it is widely thought to be in decline, the second because it has often been thought to be historically relative, and the last because the idea of progress in art in any but a very limited sense is initially very implausible.

In the last chapter, the first of these 'test cases' was considered and the conclusion emerged that there is in fact no necessary incompatibility between progress and decline, because the decline of some things can itself be interpreted as a mark of progress. But it also appears that a progressivist Hegelian interpretation of the past is not ruled out in the case of religion either. As long as a story of continuity and transformation in conceptions of the supernatural between ancient and modern worlds can be told, Hegelian philosophy of history can still be invoked, and there is indeed some reason to think that such a story can be told, even in the case of religion, because there are detectable continuities between older traditional religious mentalities and the scientistic mentality of the modern period.

It follows that a case for *radical* discontinuity in some important aspect of human experience has still to be made out before the claims of general historical progressivism can be discounted. It is at this point in the argument that morality becomes important, because it is with respect to morality that the claim of radical discontinuity has most frequently, and probably most plausibly been made. History, on this view, is the story of the appearance and disappearance of distinct moralities.

I

In arguing for radical discontinuities in the history of morality, it is not enough (despite a common assumption to the contrary) to show that there have been important differences in the moral virtues and values of different periods. A progressivist might readily accept the existence of such differences, but hold that they are to be explained in terms of inadequate values and virtues being discarded in a continuing process of enlightenment. What has to be shown, rather, is that there is at least one point in the past when the key elements in a morality collapsed or were abandoned, and where nothing plausibly thought of as an Hegelian transformation took their place.

One prominent contemporary moral philosopher who has advanced just such an argument is Alasdair MacIntyre. In his famous book *After Virtue*, MacIntyre defends the 'disquieting suggestion' that what passes for morality in the Western world nowadays is nothing more than fragments of beliefs and practices, the historical residue of an integrated moral life which took its sense from an older thought world which has ceased to exist. MacIntyre's thesis is important and interesting, and has been highly influential, but detailed consideration of it is best deferred, while we examine a still more radical thesis, that it is not some specific morality which has collapsed, but morality itself.

This is the view of an earlier philosopher and cultural theorist whose writings have come to command increasing attention —the nineteenth-century German writer Friedrich Nietzsche. Nietzsche is hard to classify. He was Professor of Philology at the University of Berne, but though he does make extensive use of his knowledge of languages, the scope of his thought considerably exceeds the normal concerns of philology. He is often referred to as a philosopher, but his style is not that of argument and analysis so much as aphorism and passionate assertion. The range of his thought, the idiosyncrasy of his style, and the diversity of his opinions give considerable scope for variety in interpretation, but here I shall interpret his writings as primarily an exercise in philosophical history. There is good reason for this interpretation. In a set of three essays, published under the title *On the Genealogy of Morals* (OGM), Nietzsche makes clear that his concern with morality is indeed the twofold one of value and genesis which I have identified at the heart of the enterprise of philosophical history. His initial interest, he tells us, was in raising questions about the value of values but this, as he came to see, was intimately connected with their genealogy. "[W]e need a *critique* of moral values, *the value of these values should itself, for once, be examined*—and so we need to know about the conditions and circumstances under which the values grew up, developed and changed" (*OGM* §6, p. 8).

His principal task, then, is to analyse an historical predicament, that of European culture, and in so doing he arrives at an evaluative interpretation of the history of Europe (though he has things to say also about the religions and value systems of the East). At the heart of this analysis is his abandonment of the Christian culture in which he had grown up. From an early age, he says, a scepticism had sprung up within him about the conventional moral wisdom of his times. This scepticism consisted not merely in atheistic doubts, which were common enough in the period in which he lived, but in scepticism about the Christian values which had accompanied the belief in God. The advent of Darwinian biology, as well as other intellectual developments had, in his view, rendered the central elements of the Christian religion, chiefly the existence of God, untenable. The important point, however, was that Darwinian biology, or any other intellectual development productive of atheism, had not arrived out of the blue, so to speak, but was the inevitable outcome of the internal logic of religion itself. Christianity had, we might say, imploded. Yet—and this was the problem with which he was centrally concerned—the social and intellectual world in which he found himself had either failed to take this crucial fact seriously, blithely continuing with a conventional religiosity, or had retreated to a comprehensive nihilism, itself the product of the self-denying, life-denying character of 'priestly' values. Nietzsche thought himself to be surrounded by a world of thought and belief, built upon the Christian religion, whose foundations had irrecoverably collapsed, but which for the most part, it seemed, proceeded as usual, unaware of the intellectual crisis at its heart. This is the point of the famous opening passage of what is perhaps Nietzsche's best-known book *Also Sprach Zarathustra*, in which a man who parades the streets proclaiming the death of God is regarded as a madman by those who hear him. Yet it is he who sees the truth and they, the comfortable and respectable, who are deluded, deluded because they think that the values of Christian morality, which is to say morality as such, remain intact. And the only extant alternative is a still more destructive nihilism, which has given up any attempt to construe human existence in terms which make it meaningful or significant.

Since for Nietzsche neither of these alternatives is satisfactory, the way out of the impasse lies in an examination of the genealogy of morals. Nietzsche does not rest content with diagnosis. Nor is he a pessimist. The collapse of Christianity and especially Christian morality is, for him, the collapse of something deeply undesirable, and the consequence of recognizing its collapse is in fact the rejection of nihilism. Nietzsche's style of 'argument', hatred of Christian values, and rejection of nihilism is made especially clear in §18 of his essay *The Anti-Christ*.

The Christian conception of God—God as God of the sick, God as spider, God as spirit—is one of the most corrupt conceptions of God ever arrived at on earth: perhaps it even represents the low-water mark in the descending development of the God type. God degenerated to the contradiction of life, instead of being its transfiguration and eternal Yes! In God a declaration of hostility towards life, nature, the will to life! God the formula for every calumny of 'this world', for every lie about 'the next world'! In God nothingness is deified, the will to nothingness sanctified! . . . (*Anti-Christ* §18, trans. R. J. Hollingdale)

Those atheists who respond to the end of Christian theology with a nihilism expressed in the familiar nineteenth-century slogan that 'If God does not exist, anything goes', effectively go on accepting precisely the worst feature of the religion they believe themselves to have abandoned. 'Anything goes' only if the death of God is a genuine cause of bereavement. What is actually called for, according to Nietzsche, is the recognition that the demise of Christianity creates both a need and an opportunity for a *Revaluation of All Values*, the title of a late projected, but uncompleted book. To conduct such a revaluation we need to look to history.

Looking to history properly obliges us to investigate the true origins of morality. Here Nietzsche calls into play his philological knowledge and employs a distinction between good and evil, the polarity characteristic of morality as such, and good and bad, an independent and earlier scheme of evaluation. In *OGM* Nietzsche finds the origins of morality in essentially non-moral aristocratic values. These do not centre on the all-important dimension of altruism—the denial of self—but on the assertion of the heroic will to power which expresses itself in magnificence and domination. Importantly, the aristocratic 'good' does not contrast itself with its opposite in terms of evil, but in terms of the bad, the ugly, the mean, or deficient. History shows that it is those who fear and hence reject aristocratic virtues who invent the notion of 'evil' to categorize their opponents. Thereby they create *morality* as we know it. He expresses this contrast between the two types of evaluation with the following parallel.

There is nothing strange about the fact that lambs bear a grudge towards large birds of prey for carrying off the little lambs. And if the lambs say to each other, 'These birds of prey are evil; and whoever is least like a bird of prey and most like its opposite, a lamb,—is good, isn't he?', then there is no reason to raise objections to this setting up of an ideal beyond the fact that the birds of prey will view it somewhat derisively, and will perhaps say, 'We don't bear any grudge at all towards these good lambs, in fact we love them, nothing is tastier than a tender lamb.' (*OGM* §13, p. 28)

The motivation of the weak lies in what Nietzsche calls *ressentiment*, a hatred and fear of power and magnificence. The morality which this *ressentiment* generates lends the greatest importance to the suppression of egoistic self-assertion, the essence of the thing that is feared, and over time this brings to the fore an ascetic ideal in which self-denial and abnegation are represented as the chief virtues, and according to which the blessed are the poor, the weak, the maimed, and the oppressed. The highest and most seductive expression of this morality is in the Christian conception of the Incarnation and Crucifixion, according to which the most powerful conceivable being, God himself, is identified with the suffering, powerless, humiliated Nazarene of the cross.

In the social and political sphere the ascetic ideal, with its elevation of the poor and powerless, in turn generates democratic egalitarianism, a public accommodation of the mentality of 'the herd'. Nietzsche has much to say about, and to condemn in, the slave mentality which self-denial and egalitarianism express, and lays the larger part of the blame on priestly classes. It is from this, rather than any narrower racism, that his anti-Semitism arises, for by his account the Jews are most notable for having made this 'priestliness' the characteristic not merely of a class but an entire nation.

However, this slave mentality, and the priestly class whose principal ambition is to promote it, contain the seeds of their own destruction. It is the intellectual outcome of Christianity that the central proposition at its heart—that God exists—comes to be seen as a falsehood. Exactly what the process is by which this comes about is not entirely clear, but in any event the consequence is that Christian morality, the highest expression of the ascetic ideal, which because of its central opposition of good and evil is to be identified with morality as such, undergoes a complete collapse. The result is an evaluative void, into which atheistic nihilism naturally steps, and it is this evaluative void which constitutes the cultural crisis, by his account, of Nietzsche's own time.

Nietzsche is here in part adopting an alternative approach to a problem inherited from Schopenhauer, whom he describes as "my great teacher". The one thing generally known about Schopen-hauer is that he was a pessimist, someone who believed that at the heart of existence is meaningless suffering and pointless destruction. His solution was at bottom a transcendent accep-tance, but Nietzsche, by contrast, believes passionately in the pos-sibility of countering meaninglessness by the assertion of a human will to power and life. In the collapse of morality the opportun-ity for a revaluation of all values arises and this revaluation can only come about by the reassertion of the will to life and power. Nihilism, then, cannot be the answer to the cultural crisis Nietzsche identifies, because no less than Christianity it fails to satisfy the most fundamental impulse of human beings—the ineliminable will to lend meaning to life and make sense of suffering. Part of the reason for the collapse of Christianity and its ascetic ideal, indeed, is the fact that while it expresses a will to nothing (also found in the Buddhist conception of 'nirvana'), it still expresses a will which cannot in reality be satisfied with nothing. The will of human beings to meaning and significance cannot be frus-trated for ever.

Where is this revaluation of values to come from? On what is it to be based? It is here that Nietzsche's most celebrated con-ception comes into play, that of the *Übermensch* ('superman' and 'overman' are the normal English translation, neither very satis-factory). The *Übermensch* abandons the dichotomy between good and evil, and thus abandons morality itself. (*Beyond Good and Evil* is the title of another of Nietzsche's works, and perhaps expresses his whole endeavour more succinctly than any other.) Reaching back to aristocratic values, the *Übermensch* is someone who through an heroic assertion of the will is able to ground his own values.

There is a superficial resemblance between Nietzsche's geneal-ogy of morals and the position of some of the ancient Greek Sophists attacked by Plato, most notably in *Republic* and *Gorgias*. (This is not wholly surprising since Nietzsche was no admirer of

Plato.) Thrasymachus (in the former) and Callicles (in the latter) contend that morality in general and justice in particular as conventionally construed are best understood as the devices of the fearful masses using strength of numbers to stifle and constrain the exploits of the strong who would otherwise be free to declare as just whatever is in their own interests. Nietzsche's position is to be distinguished from this in two respects. First, he finds the origins of justice in the attempts of the strong, not the weak. It is the strong who seek through conceptions of justice to contain the violent *ressentiment* of the herd. Second, the antagonism between aristocratic strength and populist 'morality' is not properly appreciated if it is understood, as it seems to be in Plato, merely in terms of perpetually available philosophical positions. Rather it is the product of an historical dialectic which has formed the soul of modern Europe, and which is to be grasped in the genealogy of European culture. This is why Nietzsche is contemptuous of the superficial efforts of English philosophers to write the history of morality.

An important part of the real genealogy of morals is the near total victory of the priests over the aristocrats, the self-denying over the life-affirming. This victory is only near total, however, because it is thwarted in the end by the self-destroying character of the priestly ascetic ideal which requires a constant exercise and yet cannot satisfy it. But the solution to the crisis which the destruction of the ascetic ideal brings does not lie in a simple return to (some of) the values and virtues of the ancient world, but in a revaluation of all values.

Just what this revaluation would produce cannot be said with any certainty since it too requires not just philosophical analysis or even imagination, but an historical process. Nor can much be said about Nietzsche's guesses as to the direction in which it might go, because on the positive side of his thesis he has relatively little to say. It would not be inaccurate, however, to summarize his anticipation of the world of future values as perfectionist, hierarchical and naturalistic. Each of these terms needs a measure of explanation.

First, Nietzsche is a perfectionist in the sense that he believes the value of things to lie in their being brought to perfection. Whereas Christianity had elevated the poor in spirit—the weak, the broken, the sickly, and the deformed—Nietzsche is attracted by the more ancient ideal of the beautiful, the strong, the healthy, in short, the perfected of the species. Moreover, he subscribes to another common feature of perfectionist theories of value, namely the desirability of sacrificing the less perfect to the more perfect, and this includes sacrificing lesser mortals to greater mortals. Second, though he has very little to say directly on matters of social and political organization, apart from his repeated denunciations of democratic egalitarianism—it is clear that a hierarchically structured society is one best suited to his perfectionist ideals; the most perfect can prevail only if the most fitted to rule have the power to ensure that it does. Third, Nietzsche, in common with several other nineteenth-century writers shows himself to be considerably influenced by Darwinian ideas of nature and evolution. It is in this sense that he is a naturalist, believing as he seems to, that the natural impulses of human beings, including such features as the enjoyment of cruelty and the will to domination, should be the basis of the ideal of life affirmation and the will to power. Whereas Christianity, in its doctrine of original sin, denounces human nature and promotes in its stead an ascetic ideal by which what comes naturally to human beings is to be condemned and suppressed, it is precisely in natural greatness that Nietzsche expects to see the will to life and power most magnificently expressed.

The sharp contrast between these new values and those of Christian morality might be illustrated by the following example. It is said that in the nineteenth century the Zulu king Chaka once sought to impress some Europeans by ordering a long line of his finest warriors to leap into a fire and stamp it out with their bare feet, to their great injury of course. As long as Chaka's hand was raised the warriors continued to step forward unquestioningly, and stopped only when he lowered it. Such a demonstration of power is, from the Christian egalitarian point of view, horrendous. Chaka's behaviour is that of a moral monster, and the fact that this pointless waste of human beings is unquestioned by those under his command does nothing to remedy this, but confirms only the savage and benighted condition of the culture. There is, however, another point of view, Nietzsche's perhaps, from which this episode might be thought to be a magnificent display of human will and power, whose magnificence lies in the very fact that Chaka's action, and the attitude of his warriors, constitute an assertion of will against the confines of experience, one which rejects every suggestion of mean-spirited conformity with the fear of suffering and death. All must die; such is the nature of things. But while most will cower in the face of this fact, to die willingly at the height of one's physical perfection in a manifestation of sheer power is a sort of overcoming.

Such, at any rate, is one possible illustration of the radical alternative to conventional human values which Nietzsche's 'revaluation' should be expected to produce, and it has in its favour the fact that at several points he speaks of the desirability of dying on our own terms, rather than on those the mere passage of time visits upon us. But whether or not this example captures adequately the sort of revaluation he has in mind, it represents the sort of 'thinking the unthinkable' that has been the principal attraction in Nietzsche's writings for many people. And, importantly, it consists not merely in atheistic rejection of Christian theology, something many Europeans have found easy, but the rejection of those associated Christian values which have won such a deep-seated position in European culture and which even confirmed atheists have hesitated to abandon.

In the context of our present concerns, however, the relative merits of Christian morality and Nietzsche's naturalistic perfectionism is not the central issue for examination. What we need to ask is whether Nietzsche's account of the history of morality presents us with a clear candidate for the idea of a radical historical rupture, for it is this against which the progressivist account of the past is to be tested.

II

It is worth observing here that this question has wider significance than in the examination of the claims of this one writer, because it is this aspect of Nietzsche's thought which seems to have made him most influential in recent theorizing about European culture. One prominent line of contemporary thought, shared by many philosophers and social theorists, is that the present age is best described as 'postmodernity'. By the deployment of this expression they mean to mark that we are the successors of an age and culture, 'modernity' which has undergone an internal collapse, leaving in its wake a cultural vacuum. 'Modernity' is usually identified with that period of European history which was shaped by the moral and intellectual assumptions of the late eighteenth century—a period generally known as the Enlightenment —and the cultural vacuum created by its demise is one which Marxism, structuralism, poststructuralism, deconstructionism, hermeneutics, and a number of other theoretical approaches to the study of thought and language, have sought to fill.

Though the 'project of the Enlightenment' which formed modernity is not, as most of these writers describe it, to be thought of as specially Christian, its collapse shares many of the features Nietzsche finds in the collapse of Christianity. It is for this reason that his analysis has been influential in providing a structure and a strategy for those who have wanted to analyse this other, different though related, cultural crisis. As with the demise of Christianity, for instance, the collapse of the intellectual framework of modernity sweeps away some truly foundational ways of thinking, leaving deep uncertainty and confusion. The two most notable of these are thought to be the belief in an external scientifically describable reality, and an objective order of values discernible through the exercise of universal reason. It is for this reason that social science, moral and political theory and the realm of art have been especially susceptible to postmodernist influences.

Postmodernism, then, may be said to be the belief in, or the condition of (the use of the label tends to vacillate between the two) a sort of chaos of ideas in which and with which the cultural theorist must 'play', in the hopeful expectation that new and hitherto largely unimagined avenues of thought will open up. Like Nietzsche, many postmodernists see the 'genealogy' of ideas as the most promising first step to take in coping with the collapse of modernity. Thus Marxist, deconstructionist and hermeneutic thinkers have all turned to the genesis of modernity in an attempt to see how its now discredited assumptions were fashioned. By thus understanding them in context, they endeavour to arrive at an appreciation of their limitations, and hence of the alternatives that they excluded. Like Nietzsche too, they share the ambition of 'thinking the unthinkable', of looking beyond the deep-seated presuppositions of what conventionally passes for the truth, even indeed, undermining the very idea of truth itself. Finally, also like Nietzsche, the intellectual method adopted is highly eclectic, one in which the established methods of science and social science, the familiar catalogue of philosophical problems and their analysis and the traditional distinctions between disciplines are abandoned in favour of the deployment of a battery of techniques and insights from linguistics, literature, psychoanalysis, history, and art criticism amongst others.

The theorists of postmodernism deploy the idea of a radical historical discontinuity just as Nietzsche does, and it is this idea, we have seen, which it is most important to examine for a better understanding of the nature of philosophical history. But it is also important for the understanding of much contemporary social thought. There is good reason, however, to continue to focus upon its formulation in Nietzsche's writings. This is not just because of his originality in this respect, but because the extreme eclecticism of postmodernism makes it difficult to find an alternative single and sustained version of the thesis.

III

We can return therefore to the point at which the previous section ended, but before considering directly whether Nietzsche's account of historical discontinuity can be sustained, there is one preliminary matter which, despite its importance for the cogency of Nietzsche's philosophical history, I propose to set aside with a few brief remarks. This is his use of the history of language. In OGM Nietzsche relies to a very considerable extent on the linguistic origins of some central value terms. His thesis about the conversion of 'good and bad' to 'good and evil' is defended in large part by etymology, the history of words, and much that he says in this connection is striking and interesting. However, though he lends great importance to his etymological investigations, it is not equally important to examine these claims here (a task for which I am unqualified in any case). This is because the etymology in itself, even if wholly correct, is logically insufficient to sustain his general thesis. The origins of strictly moral ideas, if by that we mean those which employ a contrast between good and evil, may indeed lie in quite different normative concepts which can be found to have preceded them. Yet it may still be the case that from these origins a new, independent and distinct, but valid, set of concepts was forged. Such, we can suppose, happened in physics and biology where the language of explanation became refined to such an extent that it constituted the emergence of a novel vocabulary, and something similar can plausibly be argued of modern legal concepts. What Nietzsche holds, however, is that the new vocabulary of good and evil is not merely the successor of the old, but at war with it, and the explanation of this conflict, if it really exists, is not merely genealogical; it lies rather with the underlying *ressentiment* which drives the modern moralist. There is thus at work in Nietzsche's history a human psychology, about which a little more will be said in due course, and it is this moral psychology, rather than the etymology, which is crucial.

Leaving etymology aside, then, let us ask whether Nietzsche's account of the collapse of Christian morality really presents us with an instance of a radical historical discontinuity. His claim can be summarized as follows: the cultural dominance of the Christian ascetic ideal in which self-negation is cultivated at the expense of the aristocratic virtue of self-assertion (the natural attitude of the strong), has come to an end. Moreover, having wholly displaced the aristocratic virtues which preceded it, the demise of this ideal leaves a cultural vacuum, to be filled only by a radical revaluation of all values. But the radical character of this revaluation represents and requires a complete break with morality, and hence can be expected to usher in an era wholly different from that which preceded it.

It is natural to respond to this claim by suggesting that Nietzsche mistakes the end of one morality with the end of morality as such. If the move from the aristocratic to the ascetic ideal is construed as the replacement of one morality by another (a construction he himself seems to put upon it here and there), the new evaluative order which he anticipates (and about which he says relatively little), could be thought not to mark the end of morality, but simply the advent of a new morality. And, in so far as this new order is recognizably a *morality* the 'revaluation of all values' cannot constitute a wholly new departure. Thus, the 'collapse' which Nietzsche believes himself to have detected is at most a change in morality more striking than many others.

The point at issue here might be expressed by deploying a distinction that Thomas Kuhn in recent years has made familiar in the philosophy of science. The larger part of scientific history, according to Kuhn, is the history of 'normal' science, in which there is a slow accumulation of data and development of theory. But there are also 'revolutions' in the history of science, when dramatically innovative theories prompt 'paradigm shifts', as, for instance, the shift from Aristotelian to Newtonian physics. These shifts are of very great importance; they prompt radical reinterpretations in a whole branch of science and turn it in new and more powerful explanatory directions. Nevertheless, though the distinction between normal and revolutionary science may be essential to a proper account of its history, what follows a revolutionary paradigm shift is still science. The shifts from Aristotelian to Newtonian physics, and from Newtonian physics to quantum mechanics may be strikingly radical departures, but taken together they tell a single story—the development of science. And so too, it might be claimed against Nietzsche, however radical a future departure from Christian morality may be, it will still be a morality, that is, the emergence of something that is recognizably a system of human values and virtues.

This response to Nietzsche's contention, however, does not give full weight to the distinction he draws between good and evil on the one hand and good and bad on the other. The new evaluative order of which he speaks is 'beyond good and evil', that is, one in which this contrast no longer makes sense. The point about Christian morality is that it invokes the idea of *absolute* values—that is what the peculiar language of good and evil signifies. These values are absolute because they are conceived as the dictates and requirements of an all-knowing and all-powerful God with whom it is senseless for human beings to contend. As the Old Testament writer of Job puts it: "This I know for the truth: that no one can win his case against God. If anyone does choose to argue with him, God will not answer one question in a thousand. He is wise, he is all-powerful; who has stood up against him and remained unscathed?" (Job 9: 2–4 REB).

In the context of this conception, the ideal of self-abnegation makes sense. Unless the finest and best in human accomplishment is constantly seen in the context of the divine, then only self-deception can disguise its gross limitations. When someone in the style of Prometheus pits his human will or reason against the gods, then however stirring an example his courage and self-assertion may be, any pride which accompanies it must be short lived. For God will not be mocked forever, and has the power to ensure that he is not. Better, then, that we should subjugate our will to his, than that we should assert it and invite disaster.

Without this background, there is, arguably, an inevitable fruitlessness about the pursuit of *absolute* good and evil, a pursuit which some have thought to mark moral philosophy in the modern period[1] and which certainly reflects an important part of its recent history. The idea of an absolute good which is not backed by the sanction of absolute power and wisdom, something which human beings individually or collectively cannot command, is thus a chimera. It did not figure in the aristocratic thinking of the Greeks, according to Nietzsche, and it cannot figure in post-Christian values either. This is the thought which makes the death of God so central a part of Nietzsche's thinking. A revaluation of all values is called for because the metaphysical basis upon which 'morality' is built has been removed.

IV

Although in many respects a radical thinker at odds with his times, Nietzsche shares with several other nineteenth-century writers a belief in the obvious intellectual demise of theology and religion. The cogency of this belief formed the subject-matter of

---

[1] See G. E. M. Anscombe, 'Modern Moral Philosophy'.

the last chapter, but what we have seen is that for one important line of thought, the decline of religion and the collapse of morality are intertwined, and for this reason some of the issues raised in the last chapter need to be touched upon again.

If the arguments presented there were correct, secularization is not a belief that can be accepted without substantial qualification and reservation. Yet, it is hard to deny that the intellectual status of theology did indeed change markedly in the course of the last century, leaving it for the most part marginal to the central issues of science, history, and politics in this one, or to deny that the nineteenth century saw a significant shift in the cultural position of Christianity and its doctrines. An important part of this change was the widespread religious disaffection of the intellectual classes of Europe, to which, of course, Nietzsche himself belonged. This resulted, however, not so much from a general secularization—the social decline of religion—but from secularism, which I earlier characterized as the belief that religion is antithetical to rational enlightenment.

Against the claims of secularists I argued that the belief in progressive enlightenment must itself retain a conception of the spiritual, the power of the mind and will to transcend the confines of naturalized explanation. At a minimum, I alleged, this opens up the possibility of, so to speak, the reinvention of God. Some prominent contemporary philosophers have in fact advanced just such a view. In his book *Sources of the Self*, Charles Taylor argues that in attempting to arrive at an adequate understanding of the self and its value, human beings inevitably yearn to accommodate moments when we "may believe ourselves to have been spoken to by angels" (p. 48), and that this is a fact which atheistic philosophies cannot encompass. There is, however, an important gap in this argument, one which Quentin Skinner powerfully uncovers in his discussion of Taylor's book.

No doubt many of us continue to feel that our lives lack sufficient meaning unless they are somehow ratified by God. But many of us have instead come to realize that, since there is no God, we shall somehow have to manage on our own. It is strange that Taylor has so little to say about this familiar but tragic element in modern consciousness . . . Taylor has plainly never suffered this depressing experience as his passing references to 'complacent agnostics' make painfully clear. It is not only evident, however, that such feelings have by now become widely and deeply embedded in our culture; it is also evident that their prevalence casts considerable doubt on Taylor's argument about the indispensability of theism. While Taylor continues to insist that the only ultimate way to satisfy our craving for meaning must be to embrace God, many of 'us' have come to recognise that such cravings will 'have' to be satisfied by whatever meanings we can find in everyday life. It is true . . . that these meanings may not amount to much; but there are no other meanings to be had. ('Who are "We"?', p. 149)

Whether Skinner accurately represents Taylor's position or not,[2] the general point, that it is illicit to argue for the actual existence of God from the desire for it, however widespread and powerful that desire may be, is a good one. Modern free thinkers can recognize the desire, even in themselves, but believe that since it cannot be satisfied, it must be lived with in other ways. And it cannot be satisfied because belief in the existence of God is not for them what William James, in *The Will to Believe*, calls a 'live' option.

We may now state more clearly the crucial question for Nietzsche's philosophical history. Is the condition in which Christian metaphysics, and with it absolute morality, ceases to be a live option, to be understood as a feature of a specific class at a particular time (nineteenth-century European intellectuals, say), or can it be attributed, as Skinner implies, to a culture as a whole? And if it can, is it possible for a dead option to come back to life? To get at these questions we need to look more closely at the idea of 'a live option' which this way of posing them employs.

---

[2] As Taylor thinks he manifestly does not. See his reply in the same volume of *Inquiry*.

Some light may be thrown on the matter by considering a fairly close parallel, that of living and dead languages. Latin is a dead language. This does not mean, obviously, that it cannot be understood, or that the literature it generated is closed to modern minds. But it does mean that it cannot be *used* in any but the most restricted sense. The reason that it cannot be used is that there exists no identifiable collection of human beings for whom it is a daily medium of expression and through whose use it is altered and adapted to meet changing needs and circumstances. By contrast, a living language does have such a use for an identifiable collection of people, though of course for many individuals and groups of individuals (perhaps the vast majority) its use is not an option, since they do not speak it, or speak it sufficiently well. Now if we draw the parallel with the Christian religion, several differences appear, but one seems specially pertinent to present concerns.

The test of a language's being dead is an empirical matter; there are or there are not natural speakers of it. We might say the same for a religion—Roman state religion, for instance—that it has no practitioners. But we cannot say this of Christianity. At no point in the last two hundred years would it have been plausible to claim that Christianity had no genuine adherents. Nor has any secularist or modern free thinker claimed this. To say that Christianity has no use, that it is not a live option, then, must be to apply a partly normative, not purely empirical test. Millions of people continue to talk the language of the Christian religion and to participate in its practices, both personally and communally. What is at issue is whether they do so to any intelligible point or purpose. There is no doubt that to modern free thinkers the utterances of Christians are unintelligible. But so too was the language of barbarians which the Greeks mistakenly identified as babble. They came to change their minds, presumably, when they saw that it was being put to some use that they could recognize.

Some features of this possibility are worth dwelling on. Some people have far less facility for the acquisition of new languages than others, and despite the near universality of English in the present day, it is probably still true that the vast majority of people have no language but their own. To them therefore the conversations and sometimes conceptions of other languages are closed. But this is a fact about them, not about their language or their culture. The transition from one language to another, it is true, may be easier or harder depending upon the degree of similarity between the two languages, but we know of no language which has completely resisted general translation into any other, whatever may be true of individual words and phrases. The reason that this is so, it may plausibly be conjectured, is that the speakers of all languages share certain common purposes as human beings which they can recognize their respective languages as serving. This, I take it, is part of the point of Wittgenstein's celebrated remark that, by contrast, if a lion could speak we would not be able to understand him.

When we turn to religion, however, the same thing cannot be said. The purposes which religion serve are widespread but not universal amongst human beings. Some people have no use for religion, as others have no use for music or fiction. To such people, religious utterances and practices will remain unintelligible, and thus for them Christianity along with other religions will not be a live option.

There is more to be said than this, however. The analysis so far would suggest that, contrary to Skinner, the idea of Christianity's ceasing to be a live option is a remark to be made about individuals and groups of individuals, not about cultures. This is not quite right however. One of the major sources of conflict which secularists usually find between religion and enlightenment is the conflict with science. It might more properly, however, be described as the conflict with technology. For most of the past, probably, the language of religion has been extensively used in the service of daily existence—prayers for rain, charms and incantations against disease and danger, appeals for divine assistance in war, and so on. If and when these uses are its principal uses, or the uses which have the greatest appeal, then, as Marx observed, the emergence of technologies ever more effective in combating the ills of this world will erode the appeal, because the use, of religion. And because Western science has enormously increased the number of such technologies, the march of modern science will bring about a decline in religious belief and practice. In short, in so far as prayers of healing or prayers for rain are employed for their efficacy, the greater efficacy of penicillin and irrigation systems will diminish the appeal of prayer.

Nearly all religions have laid great store on the practical value of prayer, worship, and sacrifice, and for any culture it could be true as a matter of fact that this is its religion's primary appeal. Skinner remarks that in the explanation of belief formation, the role of practical interest broadly understood generally plays a larger part than that of pure intellectual inquiry. If, then, the appeal of religion within a culture has rested very largely on its claims to practical mastery and manipulation, we will expect the emergence of a more successful, non-theistic rival, to diminish its stature and standing. A similar argument can be advanced which relates the explanatory power of a religion and its rivals, and perhaps yet another about the connection between religious belief and social control, the story to which Skinner is inclined to attach the greatest importance.

In the case of Christianity there is no doubt that something of this sort has happened. In both practical efficacy and explanatory power, secular technology, natural science, and scientific history have proved more successful than traditional religion, and in so far as the formation of Christian belief in the past was influenced by an interest in these, it is reasonable to expect a significant decline. The further history of the connection between Christian theology and the maintenance of social and political order is of special interest to us here. If it is true, as Skinner alleges, that "[f]riend of the mighty, persecutor of the unconventional, Christianity has at all times played a willing and crucial part in the maintenance of social control" ('Who are "we"?', p. 148), it is also true that it supplied the impetus to egalitarian individualism which has contributed to its decline. In this way, perhaps, Nietzsche's story of Christianity's implosion gains further plausibility.

However, it would be wrong to suppose that Christianity, like magic, was wholly composed of practical, theoretical and political pretensions which ultimately, it could not satisfy. Allowance must also be made for its moral and mystical components, sustained by an interest not in the practical manipulation of the human condition so much as the pursuit of meaning and value. With respect to these, science and technology have not only failed to be more successful; they cannot really be considered rivals. And many of the modern alternative political ideologies—socialism or Nazism for instance—have in most respects proved worse. More importantly, according to Taylor, nothing that secular morality has fashioned adequately addresses questions of meaning and value either.

In this assertion he may or may not be correct, and of course it is a further issue whether a return to theism could supply them by, as he puts it, holding out the prospect of "the incomparably higher". The first point of consequence here, however, is that Skinner and other modern free thinkers are in agreement to this extent; they accept that modern 'morality' is poor in comparison to what the Christians hoped for. Second, the resource to which Taylor and others turn can be construed as a theism shorn of those pretensions which have been the larger part of its undoing, and if it is, there is good reason to believe that most of the causes of contemporary unintelligibility will have been left behind. Third, to the extent that this happens the theistic spirituality that emerges will exhibit the characteristics of Hegelian transformation briefly sketched in previous chapters.

 The implications for Nietzsche's philosophical history of moral collapse, it seems to me, are these: God is not yet dead, we are not yet 'beyond good and evil', and the 'revaluation of values' which Nietzsche anticipates need not (will not?) be as radical as he himself believed. Consequently, the existence of a vacuum waiting to be filled has not been shown.

V

This is the point at which to refer again to the writings of another prominent contemporary philosopher, Alasdair MacIntyre. MacIntyre is specially interesting in this connection because he combines elements of both Nietzsche's and Taylor's lines of thought. Like Nietzsche he analyses the modern condition in terms of a drastic moral collapse, but like Taylor he sees its remedy in a return to Christian theism. In his widely discussed book *After Virtue* he begins with 'a disquieting suggestion'. It is worth quoting at some length.

Imagine that the natural sciences were to suffer the effects of a catastrophe. A series of environmental disasters are blamed by the general public on the scientists. Widespread riots occur, laboratories are burnt down, physicists are lynched, books and instruments are destroyed. Finally a Know-Nothing political movement takes power and successfully abolishes science teaching in schools and universities, imprisoning and executing the remaining scientists. Later still there is a reaction against this destructive movement and enlightened people seek to revive science, although they have largely forgotten what it was. But all that they possess are fragments: a knowledge of the experiments detached from any knowledge of the theoretical context which gave them significance; ... None the less all these fragments are re-embodied in a set of practices which go under the revived names of physics, chemistry and biology. Adults argue with each other about the respective merits of relativity theory and phlogiston theory, although they possess only a very partial knowledge of each. Children learn by heart the surviving portions of the periodic table and recite as incantations some of the theorems of Euclid. Nobody, or almost nobody, realises that what they are doing is not natural in any proper sense at all . . .

In such a culture men would use expressions such as 'neutrino', 'mass', 'specific gravity', 'atomic weight' in systematic and often interrelated ways which would resemble in lesser or greater degrees the ways in which such expressions had been used in earlier times before scientific knowledge had been so largely lost. But many of the beliefs presupposed by the use of these expressions would have been lost and there would appear to be an element of arbitrariness and even of choice in their application which would appear very surprising to us . . . Subjectivist theories of science would abound and would be criticised by those who held that the notion of truth embodied in what they took to be science was incompatible with subjectivism.

This imaginary world [w]e may describe . . . as a world in which the language of natural science . . . continues to be used but is in a grave state of disorder. We may notice that if in this imaginary world analytical philosophy were to flourish, it would never reveal the fact of this disorder. For the techniques of analytical philosophy are essentially descriptive of the language of the present . . .

Nor again would phenomenology or existentialism be able to discern anything wrong . . . A Husserl or a Merleau-Ponty would be as deceived as a Strawson or a Quine.

What is the point of constructing this imaginary world inhabited by fictitious pseudo-scientists and real, genuine philosophy? The hypothesis I wish to advance is that in the actual world which we inhabit the language of morality is in the same state of grave disorder . . . What we possess, if this view is true, are the fragments of a conceptual scheme . . . We possess indeed the simulacra of morality, we continue to use many of the key expressions. But we have—very largely, if not entirely—lost our comprehension, both theoretical and practical, of morality. (*After Virtue*, pp. 1–2)

The character rather than the cause of this moral fragmentation is moral individualism—the ascription of complete moral autonomy to the mind and/or conscience of the individual, and the relegation of the political to the social co-ordination of the potentially conflicting felt desires and self-determined opinions of individual agents. Liberalism makes a virtue of this conception of moral and political life, holds it out as the culmination of the search for freedom and enlightenment. But in fact, or so MacIntyre contends, the reality is a moral vacuum in which the crucial distinction between 'good' and 'believed to be good' disappears, and thus deprives morality, however ardently adhered to, of any rational basis.

This allegation of collapse is a less disquieting suggestion now than it was when it was made, partly because the world of philosophy is more familiar with Nietzsche than it then was. It is similar to Nietzsche's in this respect; a precondition of adequate moral understanding has, as a matter of history, been destroyed. But MacIntyre is not persuaded of the cogency, or even, coherence of Nietzsche's solution.

The attractiveness of Nietzsche's position lay in its apparent honesty . . . Since . . . the language of modern morality is burdened with pseudo-concepts, such as those of utility and natural rights, it appeared that Nietzsche's resoluteness alone would rescue us from entanglement by such concepts; but it is now clear that the price to be paid for this liberation is entanglement in another set of mistakes. The concept of the Nietzschean 'great man' is also a pseudo-concept . . . It represents individualism's final attempt to escape from its own consequences. And the Nietzschean stance turns out not to be a mode of escape from or an alternative to the conceptual scheme of liberal individualist morality, but rather one more representative moment in its internal unfolding. (*After Virtue*, pp. 240–1)

In *After Virtue*, MacIntyre proposes as his own solution to the problem a return to an Aristotelian conception of virtue. The precise details of this need not concern us here for two reasons. First, in subsequent writings this solution has been amplified, if not altogether superseded, by a return to Catholic Christianity, about which more needs to be said. Second, whatever the historical narrative which most successfully analyses the collapse of modern morality, and the moral theory which will supply an alternative conceptual framework, there is an essential practical-social dimension to any adequate solution, since "What matters at this stage is the construction of local forms of community within which civility and the intellectual and moral life can be sustained through the new dark ages which are already upon us" (p. 245).

Still, important though the practical formation of communities is, at the theoretical level MacIntyre detects an opening which may serve the restoration of coherent moral thinking. In *Whose Justice, Which Rationality?*, the second book of the trilogy which elaborates his thinking on these issues, MacIntyre records certain important Augustinian insights into the deficiency of Aristotle's moral psychology. In common with most Greek thinkers of the period, Aristotle supposes that to know the good is to will it. This raises the important, and much discussed problem of *akrasia*, or weakness of the will. If moral motivation follows automatically from knowledge of the good, how is it possible for people to know what they ought to do and yet fail to do it, which, as it seems, is a familiar feature of human experience? This problem arises, however, only if we assume that the will follows knowledge of good and bad, right and wrong. Augustine's belief, however, as interpreted by MacIntyre, is that the will is primary, and only a proper orientation of the will makes us, so to speak, susceptible to the influence of goodness. And that orientation comes from the love of God, just as perhaps we can only be influenced by those who are wise in as far as we have love and respect for them.

The merits of Augustinian versus Aristotelian moral psychology is not a topic to be examined at length here, however. Its pertinence lies in the further step that MacIntyre makes in the context of his analysis of the decayed condition of modern morality. It was, he claims, the gigantic achievement of St Thomas Aquinas to embody in a single compass these two disparate ways of thinking—Aristotle's virtue theory with Augustine's theology.

The result was a tradition of thinking—Catholic Christianity—which, though it has several rivals in the history of moral philosophy, still has the capacity to formulate and hence restore a coherent conception of morality.

I do not propose to examine the grounds for this contention, or their adequacy. My concern has only been to record the existence of a major contemporary philosopher whose philosophy exhibits features of considerable consequence in the context of the themes of this book. First, MacIntyre's philosophy self-consciously incorporates both the philosophical and the historical. Second, to a significant extent he shares Nietzsche's analysis of the modern condition, though in striking contrast he sees resources for its amelioration that Nietzsche cannot allow. Third, and most importantly, this amelioration crucially includes a return to the conceptions of religion, and in particular one highly important strand of Catholic Christianity, thereby allying MacIntyre, at least in part, with the line of thought that Taylor rather more tentatively suggests.

In Chapter 4 I argued that the death of God has been much exaggerated as a feature of modernity, and that there is something to be said in favour of the ineliminability of the spiritual as an essential category in understanding both the shape of the past and the present age. What MacIntyre's thesis suggests is that this category of the spiritual may plausibly be held to retain more elements of a more substantially traditional kind than the rather general argument I advanced implied. Unfashionable though it may be, perhaps adequately understanding the shape of the past requires us to examine elements of the original Christian conception of history with which, as I claimed in Chapter 1, philosophical history began. In discussing the shape of the past, we have so far been concerned only with, as it were, surface appearance. While exploring the idea of progress conceptualized in Hegelian terms, albeit sympathetically, no use was made of the inner dialectic of mind with itself which is what, according to

Hegel, history properly understood reveals. Hegel's conception of Absolute Mind, of course, is, within his scheme of things, the logical equivalent of God. To explore this idea properly we have now found some reason to examine the full-blown theological conception of history as the revelation of divine purpose and providence. But before doing so, for the sake of completeness, there is one more 'surface' shape to be examined, that of 'recurrence'. It is to this idea that the next chapter is devoted, before turning to an investigation of history as the outcome of providential design.

6   Recurrence

THE idea of historical recurrence has ancient roots. In the first century BC Lucretius remarked "Some races wax and others wane, and in a short space the tribes of living things are changed, and like runners hand on the torch of life" (*De rerum natura*, ii. 75). It is indeed a striking feature of history that so many cultures and empires have risen to great eminence, and then completely vanished. The world at any one point in its past has had remarkable civilizations of which there is now scarcely any trace. For instance, Charles Pellegrino writes of Agade, the ancient imperial capital built by the Akkadian king Sargon:

Agade itself is referred to in several Ur tablets as one of the most magnificent cities ever built by the hand of man. Rising from virgin, unsalted ground, it boasted the widest canals, the largest gate, the most people, and a pyramidlike temple two hundred feet wide at its base. Yet of this city, not one brick stands upon another to mark Sargon's achievements. Today archeologists cannot guess within ten miles where the king's palace once stood. (*Return to Sodom and Gomorrah*, p. 128)

Amongst ancient civilizations, Babylon is better known than Akkadia, partly because we remember its Hanging Gardens to have been listed among the Seven Wonders of the World. Yet its disappearance is no less marked. If one were to travel to the spot where Babylon is reckoned to have been, all that is on view is the ruin of a ziggurat and a few pillars. Relatively recent researches reveal that the Babylonian empire reached exceptional heights not merely in building, but in mathematics, astronomy and the complexity of its administration. Some elements of this achievement persist, perhaps, in a fragmentary influence on the modern world; serious astronomy began with the Babylonians for instance. But on the whole there is no significant remainder of what was once an exceptional cultural achievement.

Much the same may be said of ancient Egypt, Greece, and Rome, and more especially of the many other empires of the Middle and Far East—of Persia, India, China, and Japan. It is true that in respect of certain of these, there are contemporary societies which can be identified as the inheritors of important legacies from past civilizations. Modern Europe still shows some of the influence of Greece and Rome. By contrast, however, the cultural worlds of Egypt, Persia, and Babylon are for the most part utterly no more. And this is an eventuality quite at odds with the expectations of their denizens, for whom they must have seemed a near permanent feature of human experience.

These two facts—the disappearance of empires and its unthinkability for the people who lived in them—give reason for salutary thought. It is almost impossible for contemporary Western minds to envisage a future in which the civilization of Europe or the technological dominance of the United States of America have become nothing more than traces of a distant past. Like our predecessors, our experience is so permeated by our culture that we can hardly view its central features as anything but fixed parts of human life. Yet, since it is reasonable to suppose that those living at the height of the Pharaohs or the Pax Romana found the disappearance of their world just as unthinkable as we do ours, we have to allow that, despite our inability to imagine it, there may come a time when fragmentary traces of the churches and palaces of Europe, the freeways and skyscrapers of America, of transportation by car and aeroplane, computers and heart transplants, will astound distant generations as the discoveries of archaeologists have astounded us.

That this will actually be the case is, of course, a speculation for which no evidence can be assembled. There may be general inductive grounds for the belief that nothing lasts for ever, but the fact that previous civilizations have been reduced to dust is no proof that there cannot be a civilization which endures indefinitely, and for all we know the modern Western world is the one which will do so. The phenomenon of disappearing civilizations is significant not so much for thoughts about the future as thoughts about the past, and in particular for philosophies of history such as those with which we have been concerned up to this point. Theories of progress, decline or collapse, in so far as they are presented as universal histories, seem to share the assumption that the past can be treated as a single story, the story of an undifferentiated humanity, which, though it takes changing social forms, may none the less be construed as a common, human past.

This is an assumption that some philosophies of history have called into question. Most notably, perhaps, a central contention of the influential eighteenth-century philosopher of history, J. G. Herder, is that such an assumption is profoundly mistaken, because quite at odds with the facts of the past. In *Reflections on the Philosophy of the History of Mankind* (1784–91), he makes the point (with typical passion and style):

[F]rom the whole region over which we have wandered, we perceive *how transitory all human structures are, nay how oppressive the best institutions become in the course of a few generations.* The plant blossoms and fades; your fathers have died and mouldered into dust; language itself, that bond of mankind, becomes antiquated: and shall a political constitution, shall a system of government or religion, that can be erected solely on these, endure for ever? If so, the wings of Time must be enchained, and the revolving Globe hang fixed, an idle ball of ice over the abyss. What should we say now, were we to see King Solomon sacrifice twenty two thousand oxen, and a hundred and twenty thousand sheep, at a single festival? (*Reflections*, Chap. VI, Book XII, italics original)

Herder's point is that the known rise, domination, and then wholesale elimination of civilizations and empires requires us to give history a construction different to that in which there is a common, cumulative story to be told. The facts of the past, he thinks, make it plain that, as far as humanity is concerned there is (to quote the Epistle to the Hebrews) 'no continuing city'. We know that there was a time when the cultural and political pre-eminence of Rome must have wholly coloured the apprehension of both past and present for very large numbers of people, a time when, for them, the history of Rome *was* world history. Nevertheless, however deeply fixed their belief, we also know that even then there were large parts of the globe over which Rome had no influence, and that eventually a time came when both empire and culture had simply ceased to be. A striking instance of this, to which Herder alludes, is Latin. To those who spoke it, its ceasing to be a living language was, perhaps literally, unimaginable. Yet it did indeed die.

According to the standard account of Herder, he makes this observation of historical transience the basis for a relativistic account of culture, morality and religion.[1] Discontinuity means that it is inappropriate for one culture to pass judgement on another. Some commentators dissent from this interpretation, and in any case any further claims about cultural relativism may go beyond what the facts of the past warrant. There is, however, at least this to be said in Herder's favour: given the appearance and disappearance of civilizations, it takes a special effort to persist with the idea of a single human history. The difficulty is compounded by the fact that a genuine understanding of lost civilizations often seems to require imaginative entry into worlds of thought and experience so different from ours that they are largely alien. This is another feature of historical understanding

---

[1] Not all commentators have interpreted him in this way. See F. M. Barnard, *Herder's Social and Political Thought*.

that Herder wants to underline. "What (he says) should we think of the wisdom of the Egyptians, when the bull Apis, the sacred cat, and the sacred goat, were shown to us in the most splendid temples?" The mentality which made this variety of religious devotion possible is wholly removed from that of the Lutheran pastor (which is what Herder was). Countless similar examples could be given since they continually arise in the serious study of the past.

So much is indubitable, but whether such radical discontinuities outweigh the continuities which history also reveals so as to render inapplicable the very idea of a single, *human* history is an issue to which this chapter will return. For the moment we will simply acknowledge the credence which attaches so easily to Herder's contention; true universal history should not be regarded as a single development, since in reality the past comprises a series of discrete cultural episodes.

It is evidence of Herder's considerable influence that the belief in radical historical discontinuity has subsequently won many adherents amongst philosophers of history. In criticism of it it is tempting to accuse Herder and those persuaded by him of inconsistency. Does their account of world history not imply that there is no world history? The inconsistency, however, is entirely superficial. To see this we need to make explicit the distinction between a single history and a universal history. The belief that the past consists in discrete cultural episodes does not exclude the possibility that these episodes, though lacking common or cumulative *content*, have a common *structure*. If it is true that the existence and disappearance of discrete civilizations rules out a single, cumulative shape to the past, such as progress, it may still be true that all these historical episodes followed the same course. This is in fact what several prominent historical theorists have claimed. Even the bare description of items in the series which Herder employs (and which it seems natural to employ), appears to carry this implication since, by speaking of 'rise' and 'fall', it attributes a very general structural shape. If each episode in the series does indeed follow a similar course, it is open to us to say that the shape of the past is one of recurrence, the recurring pattern of the rise and fall of cultures. There is no universal history, then, in the sense that human beings do not share a common past. But there is nevertheless a single historical pattern, that of recurrent forms.

I

The conception to be explored here is sometimes referred to as that of historical cycles. Arguably, Plato held a cyclical view of history, but the names of its more modern exponents are more familiar in this connection. The Italian social and historical theorist, Giambattista Vico (1668–1744) is generally regarded as the author of the first sustained exposition of the idea. It should be recorded, however, that Vico's theoretical concerns are very wide, and their interest goes well beyond philosophical history. Although his views underwent considerable revision, the starting point of his mature writings is a dissatisfaction with Descartes's theory of knowledge, and his principal concern was to overturn the pre-eminence Cartesianism gave to science and mathematics. Vico is in many ways the founding father of the human sciences, and the value of his insights does not, perhaps, lie primarily in his account of the past. However, his thoughts here have been influential too, and in describing the *New Science* of cultural history which he aims to formulate he provides at least a succinct statement of the idea under examination here, namely a perpetually recurring pattern. "Our Science therefore comes to describe at the same time an ideal eternal history traversed in time by the history of every nation in its rise, progress, maturity, decline and fall" (Pompa, p. 127).

Despite this quotation, the context and complexity of Vico's philosophy make it difficult to attribute a single, simple view of the past to him. Commentators have disagreed as to whether the conception of "an ideal eternal history" is central to his thought, or, as Isaiah Berlin put it, "mere chaff". But more recent writers, notably Oswald Spengler (1880–1936) and Arnold Toynbee (1889–1975) have been more explicit, and made familiar the concept of repeated pattern of cultural growth and decay. It is a pattern which has widely been referred to as historical *cycles*. However, there is reason to prefer the term *recurrence*, since a cycle, strictly understood, implies a more ambitious claim about the eventual return of every point within it. Thus, economists might claim that economic history is cyclical—say, growth to boom to recession to bust to growth to boom, etc. This is a cyclical pattern properly so called because it describes the continuing story of an economy in which any point will have had set predecessors and may be expected sooner or later to return. Boom always precedes recession and will also follow it, eventually. By contrast, those, like Herder, who have been struck by the rise and decline of civilizations are impressed in part by the fact that the rise of a civilization is eventually followed by its complete demise, from which it does not rise again. A story of the birth, growth, pre-eminence, and decline of Rome, for instance, must make reference to points— the change from Republic to Empire, say—which do not return, contrary to what talk of cycles should lead us to expect. This is why the term 'recurrence' is preferable to that of 'cycle'.[2] What is recurrent is not the civilization itself, but the pattern which the histories of otherwise disparate civilizations all exhibit. A familiar analogy is found in the natural seasons—spring, summer, autumn, winter. It is an analogy that theorists of recurrence have

---

[2] To avoid confusion it ought to be noted here that Nietzsche, whom I have treated as a theorist of historical collapse, employs an idea of 'eternal recurrence', but that this is in a context and to a point quite different from the idea under consideration in this chapter.

frequently employed, and its exploration can be quite illuminating in examining the idea of historical recurrence.

Leaving aside complications about equatorial climes, the pattern of the seasons is recurring. Summer is succeeded by autumn, but will after a time return. The obvious truth of this does not mean, equally obviously, that every year is the same year, or that the summer which returns is the summer which hitherto we enjoyed. Different seeds were planted, different flowers bloomed, different crops were harvested. We might mark the distinction by saying that though the structure of each year is the same, the content is different. Suppose I plant seeds for a spectacular garden, which is indeed realized and with the advent of autumn fades and with winter withers. I might plant another garden next year and with equal success, but it is, in an obvious sense, a different garden. Nor need this be a matter of numerical difference only. I may of course plant exactly the same species of flower in just the same place and form the same pattern, in which case the difference between the two gardens could be said to be merely numerical. But if the kinds of plants and their layout, the sequence of their blooming and so on are changed, I have created a different garden in a wider sense of 'different'. Nevertheless, the structure of the history of the garden as dictated by the seasons remains the same. It is in this broader sense, I think, that theorists of recurrence have supposed successive civilizations to have had a similar structure.

The analogy of the seasons is only one. Another which has if anything been even more widely employed is the parallel between the course of a civilization and the course of a human life—birth, maturation, and death. This is the analogy Spengler finds alluring in *The Decline of the West*.

[H]uman history is the sum of mighty life-courses which already have had to be endowed with ego and personality, in customary thought and expression, by predicating entities of a higher order like 'the Classical' or 'the Chinese Culture,' 'Modern Civilization'—

a series of stages which must be traversed, and traversed moreover in an ordered and obligatory sequence . . . For everything organic the notions of birth, death, youth, age, lifetime are fundamentals . . . (Spengler, p. 3)

The analogy between a human life and an historical civilization has sometimes been taken to rather fanciful lengths, but is none the less worth exploring. The story of any human life follows a general pattern. The first part—infancy and childhood—is to be understood as a period of formation and accumulation: character is formed and skills and aptitudes in the widest sense are acquired. In adult life character and aptitudes are, so to speak, put into effect until, with old age, these accumulated powers fail, activity declines and ceases, eventually in death. But of course, though this common structure prevails, the content of each life is distinct and may be markedly different. For example, the lives of New York stockbrokers on the one hand and Kalahari bushmen on the other, both follow this pattern, but they are in most respects as unlike as can be. So too with civilizations. If the analogy holds and they too can be said to go through stages of birth, maturation, decay, and demise, this is wholly compatible with quite radical differences in cultural content.

What this shows is that recurrence, as a shape we might attribute to the past, is in principle compatible with the view that history comprises discrete cultural episodes, and at the same time compatible with the idea that there is an abstract global history to be discerned, what Spengler calls "something that is essentially independent of the outward forms". This is true, of course, only if history can rightly be regarded as revealing a repeated structure similar to the seasons and/or the stages of human life, only, that is to say, if the analogy holds. Whether it does is the question we now need to ask.

II

In fact, as we shall see, these two analogies are rather different and their applicability needs to be examined separately. Consider first, then, whether the analogy of the seasons can be extended to the course of a civilization, and this involves looking more closely at the analogy itself. What is it exactly that each year of growth, fruition, and decay has in common with the next? The answer lies in understanding a sequence, and a repeated process to which each sequence is subservient. The period from seed-time to harvest governs all, but only, those things that are subject to seasonal growth, which is to say, plants, chiefly, though also insects, and at a remove larger animals. We can explain why these things are subject to seasonal variation only in terms of their own processes of development. So, for instance, a seed germinates because of rises in temperature, and its coming to fruition relies upon an inherent potentiality which is stimulated by external factors. So too with its decay, which is prompted by the diminution of light and falls in temperature. The sequential pattern of temperature and light alters the conditions upon which changes in the thing itself depend. This explains how plants and insects may be made to germinate and flourish, or die, contrary to the seasonal pattern, when the appropriate conditions are supplied artificially. What this shows is that there is a causal, and contingent, connection between the conditions prevalent in each season and the response of plants and animals, the contingency being demonstrated by the possibility of creating artificial growing conditions.

Two points are worth stressing. First, seasons can be described in terms of changing meteorological conditions, and causal connections can be established between these and the growth and decay of plants; changes in heat and light describe the differences between seasons, but other terms describe the differences between stages of growth. Second, a law-like connection can be demonstrated between the first sort of difference and the second such that there is a relevant correlation between the two. Thus rises in temperature vary systematically with increases in plant size, the two being independent variables. What is the corresponding connection between the pattern which describes the course of civilizations and the content of their history?

Let us agree for the sake of argument that the course of civilizations can be described in terms of a pattern of growth and decline. In this case, however, both the further features required for genuine explanation seem to be absent. Vico it was who first set out the enticing ambition of discerning laws of history, which laws he thought would prove that for the course of each civilization "it had, has, and will have to be". Thus do such laws constitute the "ideal eternal history". His own account of why such laws are possible is interestingly complicated by the fact that it relies upon a special theory of knowledge to which we will return. But for the most part those who followed him have expected the laws of history to be empirically discoverable in much the way that laws of nature are. Gather enough historical fact and causal laws governing historical change will emerge by induction. As a matter of fact no such laws have been successfully formulated. Some not implausible candidates have been offered. Toynbee, for instance, in his monumental 20-volume *Study of History* claimed that the rise and fall of cultures is governed by external "challenges" to which they make "responses", but it is not hard to show that these concepts are too flexible to admit of serious testing in the light of evidence. It is like saying that plants are challenged by seasonal changes and that their development is to be explained by their response. This, so far as it goes, may be true, but it lacks any of the explanatory power that heat and light, the processes of growth and their physical interconnectedness provides.

In short, to speak of the spring or winter of a civilization turns out to be just a graphic way of describing, or summarizing, changes within it; it is not to point to the factors which govern those changes. There are no relevant historical laws. This is, it is true, a rather bald assertion, but it reflects a general consensus among historians which there is not much prospect of over-turning. The plausibility of recurrence theory, therefore, must rely upon the other analogy—the pattern of organic life—having more substance to it.

III

In examining this second analogy, it should be observed at the start that the pattern of birth, maturity, and death, though it is organic, does not have to be construed on narrowly biological lines. No doubt each human life takes this form because of gen-etic and physiological factors, but a life is also a story. So, when we write the story of someone's life, though it follows this pat-tern, the content is primarily its meaning or significance, not its biology. This way of employing the analogy of a life in the con-text of history is in fact more in keeping with Vico's original con-ception in the *New Science*. Though he speaks of laws of history, those who followed him but construed those laws on the model of laws of nature, departed from him fundamentally. Vico thought that true knowledge is that of the maker, a doctrine sometimes known as the *verum-factum* thesis. It is for this reason, he held, that human beings cannot truly understand the natural world. But they *can* know the social world which, by contrast, is of their own making.

[T]he world of civil society has certainly been made by men, and its principles are therefore to be found within the modifications of our own human mind. Whoever reflects on this cannot but marvel that the philosophers should have bent all their energies to the study of the world of nature, which, since God made it, He alone knows; and that they should have neglected the study of the world of nations or the civil world, which, since men had made it, men could hope to know. (Vico, p. 17)

In fact, he describes his new science as "rational civil theology". Whatever this may mean exactly, he intends to draw a contrast between a proper approach to the study of human society and models of historical inquiry and social understanding which, being derived from natural science, suppose that "human affairs are agitated by a blind concourse of atoms . . . [or] . . . are drawn by a deaf (inexorable) chain of cause and effect" (Vico, p. 19).

If we follow Vico in this, applying the analogy of human life to whole cultures means construing them as entities the interconnectedness of whose elements generates a distinct unity. Thus, though physical and mental development, sexual maturity, the procreation of children, the securing of the means of survival, the formation of families, and the onset of old age are all 'natural' i.e. biological elements in the existence of an individual human being, they are only properly understood as elements in a life when we grasp how they have been apprehended by the mind in the light of its conceptions and purposes, which in turn invokes the educational and cultural context of its formation. A human 'life', we might say, is a mental construct, not a causal sequence.

If we understand the idea of human 'lives' in this sense, and understand consequently that the principles by which they are to be understood are elements of mind rather than matter, the analogy with cultures is much more plausible than the simple, causal, seasonal analogy, for cultural life is also a mental construct. That is to say, it is the product of human thought and endeavour, not the outcome of impersonal forces. Yet, even if we grant the 'life' analogy a much greater initial plausibility, there are important difficulties still to be overcome. Chief among these is the criterion of identity for cultures.

A human life is certainly more than a biological sequence, but it is none the less the life of a biological organism. To ask *whose* life is being related is to ask for reference to an identifiable member of a species of animal. There is a nameable bodily person whose life it is. What is the counterpart to a human being in the case of cultures? There are, certainly, plenty of examples with labels available—European culture, Roman civilization, Ancient Egypt, the Babylonian empire—but what sorts of entities are these exactly, and what defines their boundaries?

The point can be put more plainly in the following way. We can determine when a person has been born or has died by reference to the commencement or cessation of certain biological functions, and these are datable events. If the analogy of life is to be applicable to cultures, we must be able to determine the beginnings and ends of these also. Now it would be wrong to be unduly sceptical about the possibility of doing this just because it is impossible to put a date on the birth of Rome, say, or on its demise. Though neither its beginning nor its end is *datable*, it is none the less plain that there was a time in the past when it did not exist, and a later time when it had ceased to exist. The fact that there are no precise dates available, then, does not carry the sceptical implication that we cannot speak of such a thing as Rome. However, it does imply that Rome came into existence gradually, and gradually declined and this leaves us with the question of deciding when either process can be said to have taken on sufficient solidity to allow the judgement that Rome existed or had ceased to exist.

One answer to this question is that a civilization exists as a distinct entity once all the different aspects of its culture can be interpreted as being held together by a single underlying theme or motif. This is Spengler's suggestion, and he regards it as one of the most innovative elements of his theory of history.

Present-day historians think that they are doing a work of supererogation in bringing in the religious or social, or still more art-history, details to 'illustrate' the political sense of an epoch. But the decisive factor—decisive, that is, in so far as visible history is the expression, sign and embodiment of soul—they forget. I have not hitherto found one who has carefully considered the *morphological relationship* that inwardly binds together the expression-forms of all branches of a

Culture, who has gone beyond politics to grasp the ultimate and fundamental ideas of Greeks, Arabians, Indians and Westerners in mathematics, the meaning of their early ornamentation, the basic forms of their architecture, philosophies, dramas and lyrics, their choice and development of great arts, the detail of their craftsmanship and choice of materials. (*Decline of the West*, p. 191, emphasis original)

Spengler refers to this idea as the morphology of culture. Morphology in this sense is the cultural manifestation of an underlying fundamental idea or sets of principles. It is one worth examining, though Spengler himself takes it to points that some have thought absurd. Who amongst traditional historians, he says,

realizes that between the Differential Calculus and the dynastic principles of politics in the age of Louis XIV, between the classical city state and the Euclidian geometry, between the space perspective of Western oil painting and the conquest of space by railroad, telephone and long range weapon, between contrapuntal music and credit economics, there are deep uniformities? (*Decline of the West*, p. 192)

There does seem to be something fanciful and extravagant about the suggestion that things as diverse as differential calculus and dynastic politics should be reflections of one and the same thing. But even if it is agreed that Spengler takes his belief in underlying, unifying conceptions to excessive lengths, plausible examples of the idea of morphology with which he is working can still be found. Take, for instance, the case for individualism as the underlying idea of modern Western culture. It may be fanciful to construe contemporary mathematics or building techniques as expressions of the individualistic ideal, but it is not difficult to see concern with the individual dominant in much modern European philosophy, painting, literature, morality, economics, and political theory. Moreover, it is this concern with the individual which provides a notable contrast between post-

Enlightenment Europe and the cultures of the ancient world, the Far East, and mediaeval Christendom. If we add that historical inquiry reveals a gradual development of this concern throughout the eighteenth and nineteenth centuries, and further speculate on the significance of a return to more communitarian themes in the era of 'postmodernism', we have gone far towards assembling the elements of a distinctive cultural morphology.

But just how discrete is the culture we have here described? Discreteness, let us recall, seems essential to the conception of historical recurrence we are exploring. It is only if cultures are discrete that we can find in them a repeated 'ideal eternal history'. Close historical inquiry, however, usually undermines claims to cultural discreteness by uncovering continuities which the use of labels such as 'ancient', 'mediaeval', or 'modern' tend to disguise. Modern Western culture may indeed have been dominated by the idea of the individual, but the origins of this concern are to be found in early Christianity and in classical Greece and Rome. There is in fact a large measure of continuity between our culture and the cultures which preceded it, and in recounting the move from one to the other we have to acknowledge long periods of overlap. Something of the same may be said in other contexts; to understand communist China, especially under Mao, we need to see it as the descendant and inheritor of an Imperial past, a culture which, despite many important differences, retained significant elements from its past. In most cases, in fact, the inquiries of cultural history reveal the past to be more a process of gradual transformation than a series of discrete episodes. There will, it is true, be periods in this process when certain ideas and conceptions are sufficiently dominant to allow the uses of names and labels which capture markedly distinguishing features between cultures; terms such as 'Classical Rome' and 'mediaeval Europe' are neither useless nor wholly mistaken. But there is a clear and considerable leap required before we can move from speaking in these ways to the much more ambitious thesis that history can be divided into separate epochs or discrete civilizations. Even between otherwise largely distinct cultures there are often connections and continuities. Arguably, for instance (though the evidence is inconclusive), Mahayana Buddhism is the outcome of the impact of early Christian missionaries on the original Theravadin form.

What these reflections suggest is that the analogy of life deployed with respect to cultures fails because we cannot demarcate or separate cultures as we can separate the lives of individual human beings. And if we cannot do this we do not have any potential exemplars of an ideal recurring pattern.

But even if we did, there is a further problem which the recurrence thesis encounters. This is similar to the objection which was earlier brought against the seasonal analogy. Is there an explanatory connection between the recurring pattern and the civilizations which undergo it? Or is the pattern merely a shorthand way of describing the changes which civilizations have, as a matter of fact, undergone? The maturation of a human being takes the form of accumulating personal abilities, experiences and social attributes. These are explained by underlying physiological and psychological processes which can be described independently of the personal histories of different individuals. To say this is not to subscribe to some form of reductionism, according to which a human life is merely the development of a biological organism. Physiology and psychology do not genetically *determine* the course of each life, but they make such a life possible and explain its general pattern. What is the counterpart to these processes in the case of civilizations? In Vico there are the elements of an answer in the idea of a collective human consciousness. Early stages of history, for instance, are on his account driven by a 'poetic' mentality. Something of the same sort is found in Comte. But the introduction of these ideas hugely complicates the theory. On the other hand, if we stick to the relatively more simple conceptions of Spengler or Toynbee, there does not seem to be any counterpart. The recurrent pattern, in so far as there is one and in so far as it is found in different civilizations, is just that—a pattern. In similar fashion we can find an ideal pattern which every snowflake tends to have. But we have explained the form of snowflakes only when we have uncovered the physical processes which explain the pattern. In the absence of some counterpart to this, the belief of Spengler, Toynbee, and others (Marx, possibly), that they had formulated, or begun to formulate, *laws* of history, was mistaken; they had at best discerned descriptive *generalizations*.

IV

Neither of these objections, however, destroys completely a conception of the shape of the past as historical recurrence. With respect to the first—the absence of discrete civilizations or culture—it might be replied that even if civilizations cannot be thought of as wholly discrete, wherever there is a sufficient distinction between them to allow us to attribute them separate identities, we can still subject them to analysis in terms of morphological structure. This is what we do with religions for example. Judaism, Christianity, and Islam have common features, and internal variations, but we are not thereby inhibited from identifying them as distinct religions, each characterized by leading conceptions and ideas which serve to explain the various forms in which they have found expression. With respect to the second objection, it might be replied we have not taken seriously enough Vico's insistence on the impossibility of explaining human affairs "by a deaf (inexorable) chain of cause and effect". The cogency of the objection relies too much on the causal conception of explanation, which was itself rejected in the connection with the seasonal analogy. Rather we should replace the causal paradigm by interpreting the parallel between the life of a human being and the life of a culture in terms of the concepts of narrative and story.

Here it is worth recalling some of the points made in Chapter 2. Narrative structure explains the content of a story by providing criteria of relevance and significance, not by revealing the underlying causal processes which make it possible. The most familiar pattern of narrative—beginning, middle and end—establishes internal relationships of intelligibility between passages within it and thus establishes the mark of its completion. Thus, in writing a political biography, for example, an author tries to discern the beginning of a career, the actions performed in bringing it to fruition and the nature of its conclusion in terms of the success or failure of its ambitions. In this way, we explain the life by making sense of it, not by identifying its necessary and sufficient conditions, or the causal laws which controlled it. Why cannot we do the same for, say, the rise and fall of the Roman empire?

One reason for continuing to think we cannot do so might be thought to lie with the first of the two earlier objections. The life of a politician has a unity underlying it, when it does, because it is the life of one person. It is one person's ambitions, career, actions, and accidents. In other words, it is the life of a single agent. The trouble with trying to do the same for cultures is that, in the absence of illegitimate anthropomorphizing, there is no single agent whose life it is. People sometimes speak of, for example, the spirit of the Renaissance as though it were a controlling agent, but this is at best a helpful metaphor.

However, just how great a difficulty is the absence of a single agent? Can we not make do with an informing principle which is not a 'spirit' in any stronger, anthropomorphic sense? Consider an instructive, and possibly bridging case—that of musical styles.

The periods into which the history of Western music may be divided share several of the features that mark divisions into cultural periods. Renaissance, Baroque, Classical, Romantic, and Modern are all labels that capture distinctive but not discrete periods. Between any one and the next in the sequence there is considerable overlap. Nevertheless, an informed ear can place most compositions in one or other period. Furthermore, musical analysis can uncover in each an underlying unifying principle of composition. There is, of course, a very great deal to say about these principles, far more than could be discussed or even recorded here. But it is possible, even briefly, to identify plausible governing conceptions for each of them. Thus, for example, there is reason to hold that while Baroque music seeks the construction of harmonic order, Classical music exploits musical form, and Romantic music strives for musical expressiveness. These are, of course, drastic simplifications and in any case the three are not exclusive. But they serve to make the following relevant points.

1. The composition of Baroque music clearly began, developed, matured, and faded, even though we cannot put precise dates on any of these phases and can trace significant connections with the music that came before and after it.

2. Though it was not the work or ambition of any one composer, or even of composers otherwise related to each other, there is a detectable unity to it.

3. This unity can be identified with a nameable principle or set of principles of composition.

4. It is natural to describe the phases through which it went in terms of the 'life' analogy. Historians easily and intelligibly speak of such music as being 'in its infancy' or 'reaching a greater maturity'.

5. The story of its rise and fall is the story of a new musical potential, developed and exploited to the point at which it was exhausted. This is why, though it is perfectly possible to compose in the Baroque style now, any such composition cannot but have the character of imitation or pastiche.

6. We can meaningfully mark this fact by saying that there is no life left in the Baroque; that as a mode of composition it is dead.

The intelligibility and substance of all these ways of talking is sufficient to show that the 'life' analogy, and the hypotheses and analyses it gives rise to, retain a plausibility and usefulness even when applied to contexts that show serious disanalogies with the lives of human beings. And in so far as what has been said here about Baroque can also be said about Classical and Romantic, the idea of a recurrent structure repeated in historical sequence also gains plausibility, though it has to be noted that the parallel is less than perfect, since while from the point of view of composition these styles are dead, from the point of view of listening and performance they are as accessible as ever they were.

V

It remains to ask whether the case of musical styles, in which unity without independent agency is exhibited, does indeed supply a bridge which will enable us to extend the talk of birth, maturity, decline, and so on, to cultures more broadly conceived. To begin the process of extension we can usefully stay with the Baroque. This is because the label 'Baroque' has been widely applied to more than music—architecture for example. Can we find a larger underlying principle or conception which will reveal a unity between the composers and the builders of the period referred to in this way? Despite the extended use of the label, it is not easy to see how this can be done, though if Spengler were correct, this ought to be amongst the least difficult cases. In his usual style he himself is in this case optimistically ambitious and sees a clear relationship between "the social polish of the period", "the fugues of Bach", "the vase-paintings of Exekias", and "French conversation", all of which, he claims, presuppose "a strict and carefully matured convention and a long and exacting training of the individual" (*Decline of the West*, p. 135).

But once again we need not follow Spengler's extravagance. We need not even puzzle unduly over the difficulty of finding a connection in what ought to be an easy instance, because even if we could, the difficulties we will encounter in trying to do the same for other periods are far greater, and seemingly insuperable when we turn to wider aspects of culture. In fact, even if we restrict the range of cultural reference very greatly, the sort of cultural unity which the theory of historical recurrence requires will not be forthcoming. Take for instance, nineteenth-century Britain, commonly called the Victorian period. There is no doubt that certain common attitudes and beliefs marked this period. Nor is it fanciful to see Victorian politics, commerce, technology, and ideas about personal morality all infused by a liberal progressivism which emphasized the importance of individuality, freedom, and social development. What is less plausible is the extension of this general theme to other important cultural aspects of the same period. In religion, for instance, Victorian England was notable for two dominant influences—the impact of science and the rise of Anglo-Catholicism, neither of which has any obvious connection with liberal individualism. In the arts, too, the dominant influences appear to lie elsewhere. Music and poetry were influenced by an expressive Romanticism which tended to be anti-bourgeois, and in the second half of the century architecture came to be dominated by the backward looking neo-Gothic movement. To follow the story of Victorian England is to record the disparate influences of a deeply interesting age, but it is not to follow the development, outworking, and exhaustion of any one idea, or even set of ideas. There is indeed reason to regard Victorian England as the high point of a certain sort of liberalism, a philosophy which, by way of municipalism, gave rise to the socialist orientation of the twentieth century, but if so, this is true of what is generally known as public life, not of the culture as a whole.

Once we turn to something larger yet—European culture—the conflicts and disparities are greater yet. Arguably, the dominant political theme in the continental Europe of the nineteenth century was the rise of nationalism and the demise of imperialism, a view confirmed in part by the strikingly different terms in which the political boundaries of Europe were settled following the Congress of Vienna (1815) and a century later, after even greater international conflict, by the Treaty of Versailles (1919). While the former concerned itself entirely with an imperialistic 'balance of power', the latter took up the application of the 'self-determination of peoples'. It can also plausibly be argued that nationalistic aspirations had an influence on both music and the social sciences; Verdi, for instance, became something of a symbol for Italian nationalists, as Wagner did for the German nationalists, and the emergence of linguistics undoubtedly had much to do with an interest in ethnicity. But nationalism had virtually nothing to do with the staggering changes in science and technology which took place in Europe at the same time, save where these were driven by the arms industry. *Pace* Spengler, the growth of the railways had almost everything to do with commercial opportunities and developments in engineering, and nothing much to do with conceptions of space and time, still less nationalistic ones. Conversely, the refinements in science which explain these developments share little common ground with the world of the arts where the emphasis was increasingly on the romantic, partly perhaps in reaction.

These are all assertions about the actual course of history, and as such, since they are contestable, cannot stand as a conclusive refutation of the recurrence theory. With sufficient ingenuity, recurrence theorists such as Spengler might manage to find resonances and similarities, which they could claim (as Spengler did claim) lay beneath the surface story with which more ordinary historians foolishly rest content. It is a matter of judgement as to whether and when such ingenuity ceases to be insightful and becomes merely fanciful, a line which Spengler, for all his great learning, is generally thought to have crossed. But the main point to be made is that the recurrence theory, of Spengler or of Toynbee, must answer to historical fact, and only to historical fact. Even if, as I have argued, a sympathetic exploration of the 'life' analogy shows it to be more plausible and applicable to cultures than may at first appear, there is a good case to be made for the contention that the history of any period is too diffuse and varied to allow the systematic application of any such analogy.

In this the theory of recurrent historical cycles differs from the other theories we have considered. Theories of progress, decline, and collapse are essentially normative. Although they too must sooner or later 'fit' the facts of history, their strictly normative elements give them an independence which allows for a different sort of interpretation of history. A theory of progress, for example, can 'fit' an awkward fact to its conception of the past by interpreting it as evidence of temporary regression. In this way the theory has a means of attributing significance to the facts of the past that is to a degree independent of their limited historical significance, which is to say their immediate contextual significance and the arguments for this attribution have to do not with historical fact alone, but with the normative concept of progress. Recurrence theory, by contrast, does not enjoy this advantage. It is, in the end, a descriptive theory which aims to generalize about the actual structure of the periods of the past. As a result, the only way in which recalcitrant facts can be accommodated is by making ever more general the categories which the theory employs. Thus, to take Toynbee's terminology, as historical evidence mounts the categories of 'challenge' and 'response' become ever more abstract and flexible. In doing so they lose whatever analytical value and explanatory power they might have had. As the argument of this chapter has shown, the idea of a unifying principle which explains the course of a culture in terms of birth, development, maturity, and decay, *could* be an accurate account of how the past has been; unfortunately, it seems to have been only partially and spasmodically how it *was*.

The conclusion must be that though recurrence theory is not

as foolish or fanciful as it has generally been regarded, it fails as an account of the shape of the past. Such plausibility as it has rests upon the idea that what Spengler calls 'world-history' has a narrative rather than a causal structure. That is to say, the events of history are not to be related merely as a sequence where one event leads to another in accordance with causal laws which history or social science might both formulate and deploy, but in a story, told in terms of beginning, middle, and end, origins, development, and denouement. In Spengler, as in Vico, this narrative structure arises from the man-made character of the past. There is, however, a yet more ambitious, and older, narrative which the past has been thought to embody. This is the idea of the past as a story of the designs and intentions of a divine Providence, and it is to this, the final 'grand' conception of the past to be examined, that we now turn.

7 Providence

VICO, some of whose ideas were considered in the last chapter, differs from most other recurrence theorists in this respect if no other; he seems to have believed in the historical importance of Divine Providence. It is debatable just how far the idea of God's plan for humanity really figured in his theory of history. Perhaps its appearance has something to do with the constraint he felt under to show that his ideas were consonant with the prevailing Christian orthodoxy of his day. Taken at face value, his writings do attach considerable importance to theological conceptions, and there is no reason to doubt his own religious conviction. On the other hand, at points, the sheer effort he makes to bring Providence into the story at certain points suggests that he may have been motivated by factors other than the search for philosophical adequacy. His description of the *New Science* as "rational civil theology" does little to resolve the matter. Perhaps its being a "civil" theology implies that the normal concepts of divinity can be suspended; perhaps its being a "theology" implies that God is to be given an essential role.

This is an issue, in all probability, which the evidence of the text cannot settle, but in any case it need not specially concern us here. If we ignore his motives and concentrate on the internal logic of his theory, more substantial doubts about the role of Providence emerge. It is not the purpose of this chapter (or indeed the previous one) to offer an exposition of Vico, still less a summary, partly because his rather diffuse writing gives rise to large and complex issues of interpretation. However, it would not be inaccurate to say that one of the most important of these is an ambiguity with respect to the role of Providence. The section of *The New Science* entitled 'The first principle of nations is providence' begins: "Now to commence these principles with that idea which is paramount to any work whatsoever, the architect of this world of nations is divine providence. For men cannot join together in human society unless they share a human sense that there exists a divinity who sees into the depths of their hearts" (Pompa, p. 104).

The reason for this, according to Vico, is that only thus will they have sufficient motivation to keep the agreements they make with each other. But does Vico mean to assert here the importance of *God* in history, or the importance of *religious beliefs about God*? If the latter, while both the belief in God and the different ways in which human beings have formed ideas of God are essential to the historical process, God as providential agent drops out of the picture.

Vico, then, cannot be regarded as an unambiguous proponent of the idea of God in history, but if we are looking for a view of the past in which Divine Providence plays a central part, there are many less ambiguous instances. Some of these are very ancient. As we saw in Chapter 1, large parts of the Old Testament comprise a sacred history properly so called, in which the course of the past is explained by the actions and intentions of God. Old Testament sacred history is not exactly theoretical; it employs, but does not explicitly elaborate, religious or theological concepts of historical analysis and explanation. The same is true of its Christian descendant, at least in its early stages. The New Testament affirms God's saving actions in history, but has relatively little to say about the nature of explanation and the role of evidence which this affirmation implies. These issues do get treated in subsequent Christian theology. Both Eusebius (d. AD 370) and St Jerome (AD 342–420) are early Christian writers who exhibit a special interest in the historical nature of the Christian revelation, but it is most clearly St Augustine who first saw the necessity of a distinctively Christian interpretation of the past, one which would counterbalance the 'pagan' history generally accepted in his own day. At first he assigned the task of constructing a salvation history to a refugee protegé, Orosius, but the increasing importance he attached to it is reflected in the fact that he eventually took over the work himself. It is in his monumental *City of God*, to which he devoted many years, and especially in its later books, that the fundamental ideas of a theologically driven universal history are first expressly explored. Indeed, as was noted earlier, it is to Augustine that we owe the very term 'sacred history', and according to the historian Herbert Butterfield "his book must remain—outside the ancient Scriptures—the supreme example for study if one is interested in the connection between history and belief". (Butterfield, p. 125. Despite this remark, Butterfield holds "it was Orosius rather than Augustine who influenced the succeeeding centuries".) Even so, the idea of a theory of history such as came to be familiar in the nineteenth century is largely implicit rather than explicit in Christian no less than Jewish sacred histories, including Augustine's.

This is why the principles of sacred history have, in the main, to be elicited from instances of this way of thinking, though some of Augustine's more self-conscious ideas are worth examining. Eliciting these principles is the first aim of this chapter, an essential preliminary to examining the problems which such principles encounter, which will in turn allow us to take some view of the plausibility to be attributed to the idea of a sacred history.

I

In undertaking this task there is a danger of being so overwhelmed at the outset by longstanding conceptual and philosophical problems that the enterprise proper never begins. To take just one obvious example. Ascribing a role to God in history implies that

God exists. But does he? Some of the theories considered so far have employed entities—cultures and civilizations, for example —over whose interpretation disagreements and uncertainties easily arise. 'What exactly is a civilization?' and 'What implications does the talk of civilizations have?' are real questions, but no one seriously doubts that such things exist or have done so in the past. By contrast, this is precisely what very many people *have* doubted in the case of God. Of course, the number of religious believers and theologians who have set themselves to answer these doubts is not any smaller, and the debate between the two groups has continued over a long time. The result is that the relevant issues involved in asking this seemingly straightforward question have become very large and complex, without, however, their elaboration producing any very general philosophical consensus.

The question of God's existence is plainly crucial to the truth of most sacred histories; if God does not exist, sacred histories are false. But its proper consideration would postpone indefinitely the discussion of matters directly relevant to the idea of sacred history itself. We must, therefore, take the same approach here as over the metaphysical debate between Idealism and Realism, namely note its importance and set it on one side. Nor is the existence/non-existence of God the only problem connected with the idea of a sacred history of which a similar view must be taken. Even those who agree that God exists may hold that there are deep difficulties with respect to his nature in its implications for history. For example, how can a being whose eternity requires him not to be in time and space none the less bring about effects in time and space? If God is not in time, he cannot act in time; if he can act in time, he is not 'beyond' time. Or so it seems reasonable to suppose. This is another question that has long occupied metaphysics and philosophical theology, and as in the first case, it would be impossible to take a considered view on it, or even explore it adequately, in this limited context. So it too has to be left to one side.

There are in fact a great many such questions, not all of them

strictly philosophical. One further important issue is the authority of Scripture. All Jewish and Christian sacred histories (and it
is these two with which I shall be primarily concerned) seem to
take it for granted that the Bible is the revealed word of God.
Without this, the enterprise would appear to be baseless. Yet it
is an assumption which many people, including some believers
in God, do not see reason to make. On what grounds, if any, is
it to be defended? This is an important question, and one which
cannot be set on one side as easily as can those of metaphysics.
It is a subject to which we will have to return, but in order to do
so profitably, some considerable stage-setting is required.

Since the metaphysical questions are highly vexed, they alone
would in any case seem to present major obstacles to proceeding with the direct investigation of sacred history. Will it do simply to suspend them? In fact, the recommendation that they be
left aside is not specially disabling, nor is it uncommon in philosophy, whose concerns are so deep and far reaching that something of this strategy is almost always required. In this particular
case, however, it takes a special effort to suspend the questions
of God's existence and his nature, since both seem so central to
the plausibility of sacred history. But it may help to observe that
though God's existence is a *necessary* condition of the truth of
any sacred history, it is not *sufficient*, and the central topic to be
explored here is whether, if he does exist, he can usefully be
invoked in the interpretation of the past.

To appreciate this point we have only to recall the distinction
between deism and theism. Deism is the view that God exists,
and was responsible for the creation of the world, but for the
most part leaves it to its own devices. This is consistent with
occasional interventions, but such interventions will be, so to
speak, one-off events which have no special significance in understanding the shape of the past as a whole. Thus, though the deist
God might perform an occasional miracle, this would at best be
of limited significance. On this understanding of his activity, God

might, for instance, choose to bring about the miraculous cure of a prince or emperor and thereby perpetuate his rule for a time. But the underlying explanation of the survival of his empire would still lie with the political, economic and social forces of the period. God would have intervened in the course of events, but would not have controlled or determined their general course. He is, to this extent, no different from any other agent.

The theistic God, by contrast, not only created the natural and social worlds, but is constantly at work in them. Such is Augustine's God, for it is clear that Augustine had a very strong sense of the agency of God in everything, from the world-historical to the everyday. More is to be said about this, but what the distinction between deism and theism shows is that the *existence* of God is not the only issue that might be the undoing of sacred history.

Clearly, if what has been said in the last few paragraphs is correct, it is theistic conceptions which must underlie a sacred history. Acknowledging this raises further questions, as Augustine himself realized. If God is at work everywhere and in everything, what is the mark of those events which offer special evidence of his providential design? Given that what sacred history aims to uncover is the hidden meaning of events, hidden, that is to say, from those who, in the style of the pagans, concern themselves only with recounting sequences, are we to suppose that all events have hidden meaning, or only some? And if all, is the meaning of each equally significant from the point of view of world history? Second, how is hidden meaning discerned? Can it be discerned by anyone, or only those possessed of some special sort of perception and understanding? Third, what is the means or mechanism by which God effects his purposes, and how does this relate to their meaning? Does an historical event have theological meaning just because God brought it about, or do we need to know why he brought it about? These are all important questions to which the idea of a sacred history must supply answers if it is to be coherent, and it must do so even if the other, perhaps more profound, theological and metaphysical questions have been answered in the affirmative.

II

The simplest procedure for beginning to address these issues is to return to the Old Testament and recount one example of a sacred history. In broad outline, the historical and prophetic books of the Old Testament tell a story of the relationship between Jehovah, or more accurately Yahweh, and one set of people, the Jews. This relationship is a sort of contract, or covenant, in which each of the parties pledge themselves to the other. Yahweh chooses the Jews as the people through whom his will for the world will be revealed and realized; the Jews trust to Yahweh as the one who will, if they are faithful, bring them through trials and tribulations to a Promised Land in which the condition of Paradise, lost at the Fall, will be restored. Two sets of events may be said to make up this story. The first comprises the deeds of Yahweh; the deliverance of the Hebrews from bondage in Egypt, the provision of the Ten Commandments and the Law, the establishment of a royal line, and the return from exile are major instances. The second consists in the responses of the Jews—the rejection of graven images, the preservation of the Ark of the Covenant, the building of the temple in Jerusalem. The story of this relationship is of course a chequered one. Yahweh requires his law to be observed unfailingly, and worship to be reserved exclusively for him, and the Jews constantly prove unfaithful in both. The result is another two sets of significant events. On the one hand, as a consequence of their faithlessness the Jews are regularly visited by disasters both natural and political; on the other, Yahweh continues to reveal his will to them, and to renew his promise, through a long line of prophets. This story is set to continue indefinitely, until Yahweh brings it to a conclusion in his own good time, but there is also present in the sacred history an account of the form this end will take. The collaborative contract of Yahweh and the Jews will come to fruition with the appearance of a Messiah, a Jew specially appointed by Yahweh, who will lead the nation to its final and everlasting salvation.

This is, of course, a very broad outline of the story. There are complications in the covenant between Yahweh and Israel, and not infrequent uncertainties about the relationship between collective religious commitment and more free-standing, nationalistic aspirations. This is why it is possible for contemporary Zionism to take a non-religious form and for enthusiastic supporters of the modern state of Israel to be described as 'secular' Jews. Judaism as we now know it is not exclusively committed to one, or any, sacred history.

But we can leave this complication aside. Traditional Judaism is bound up with a sacred history and on the strength of this example it is possible to set out some pertinent general features. First, its account of the past takes the form of a narrative, a story within which events are strung together in such a way as to make them parts of a recountable whole. Second, there are two sorts of agent at work in the story— the divine and the human. Third, the role of each of these is different—the divine takes the initiative, the human responds. Fourth, there are 'key' episodes in the story, events (such as the deliverance from Egypt) which combine great human significance with divine intention.

These same features are to be found in Christian sacred history. Although an unmistakeable descendant of Judaism, the Christian narrative of the past is importantly at variance with it. There are structural similarities, but the content is different. To begin with, Christian sacred history is more properly universal, having to do with humanity as a whole and not merely some subset of it. Certainly, the history of the Jews is of special importance even to Christians (as to Muslims also), since it is here that we most clearly find God's purposes revealed, but they are his purposes for humankind as a whole. However, this difference ought not to be exaggerated. It is significant that in the Jewish version no less than the Christian, Adam is the first man and not merely the first Jew. Indeed it is this element of universalism, according to Butterfield, that marks off sacred from more ordinary histories.

It has generally been the case, and it has remained substantially the case, that the men who write political history set out to tell the history of their own state, their own city, their own nation. It is from religious or quasi-religious ideas that there springs the desire to see the human race as a whole and to envisage universal history. (*Writings on Christianity and History*, p. 114)

Still, he goes on to add, "starting in the manner I have described, Christianity gave great impetus to this notion of universal history".

A second point of difference is this. Christian sacred history is the story of salvation. Although its origins are in Eden, Augustine echoes a familiar thought when he claims that history proper does not begin until the Fall. It is the rupture between God on the one side and the human beings he has created on the other which brings about the necessity of restoration and since this is what history is all about, the Fall is when history begins. Third, the events of the Jewish nation, though revelatory in their way, are not 'key' events in the story. Augustine, in common with earlier and later Christian writers, divided history into six 'ages'. The number probably reflects the influence of the creation story, for the seventh, and final, age, inaugurated by the Second Coming of Christ, is an historical version of the seventh day in Genesis when, creation having been completed, God rested. In fact, the divisions between the first six ages do not really signify. They end with the Incarnation of God in Christ, the most decisive event of all. Everything before this is a preparation, and everything subsequent to it, however long it may last, forms an intervening waiting period before the final consummation. The consequence is that there are really only three truly key events in Christian sacred history—the Fall, which was the very cause of history itself, the Incarnation which constitutes God's personal participation in the process of salvation, and the Second Coming when the verdict of the Last Judgement completes the story.

It is worth observing that the inclusion of the Second Coming, a future event, as one of the 'framework' events in the story of salvation, shows that Augustine's conception of sacred *history* (despite his being the inventor of the expression), might more properly be called a conception of sacred *time*. For this reason it is to be distinguished from those other 'shapes of the past' with which we have been concerned so far, and which do not have this transcendental character. One implication of this is that, of the key events in the story of salvation, only two—the Fall and the Incarnation—are properly speaking historical, and it might seem that such a sparse set of events is too skeletal to provide us with even the outline of a universal history. What allows it to do so, however, is the 'plot' within which these events take on such very great significance. If we follow Augustine's particular version of Christian salvation history (most of which will be found in Books XV to XVIII of the *City of God*), this plot is the story of two cities, the heavenly city of God and the earthly city of men. History, on his account, is the story of their entanglement and gradual disentanglement, revealed in the history of the Flood, Abraham's foundation of Israel, the prophets and the kings, which events, taken together, constitute the historical preparation for the Incarnation in Christ. Augustine's two cities are societies of human beings distinguished by their spiritual, that is moral and mental, orientation. One, the members of the heavenly city, are those "who live according to God's will" (Book XV, Chap. 1). Since the divine reality is only partly experienced on earth, they are accordingly, as he says time and again, *pilgrims* in this world, seeking a final home not here but in the immediate presence of God, which is to say, in a world yet to come. The other society, the members of the earthly city, are those who "live by human standards" and consequently find themselves at home in this world with its essentially human purposes and values. History, we might say, is the story of the sifting and filtering by which the two are finally distinguished sufficiently clearly to allow for their permanent separation. The Fall represents their initial entanglement; the Incarnation and Resurrection constitute God's decisive intervention on behalf of the aspirants to the heavenly city; the Second Coming and Last Judgement confirm the completed process.

Why should we think of this as an historical process? Why, that is to say, is the story of salvation not a story repeated again and again in the lives of individuals, but without any significant historical dimension? The answer seems to be that certain historical figures are archetypes who have existed at particular times but are also symbolic manifestations of aspects of the history of the heavenly city which prefigure the purer representation of this in Christ. Thus, for instance, "David marks the beginning of an epoch, and there is with him what may be called the start of the manhood of God's people" (*City of God*, Book XVI, Chap. 43). Here we see that the reign of David is both an historical episode and a symbol. In his remarks about Noah, the Ark, and the Flood, Augustine makes this double character of historical basis and symbolic value even plainer. "No one ought to imagine that this account [of Noah and the Flood] was written for no purpose, or that we are to look here solely for a reliable historical record without any allegorical meaning, or, conversely, that those events are entirely historical, and the language purely symbolic . . ." (*City of God*, Book XV, Chap. 27).

It is not hard to understand why he insists on both dimensions. The recounting of mere history has no relevance for the conduct of existence. On the other hand, the symbolic portrayal of types, even in some sort of chronology, carries no authority, unless they are affirmed as real episodes in history. If Noah or David is held out merely as a symbolic type to which we might at any and every time aspire, there is no progress in the human attainment of the heavenly city. It is only if they are real existents that there is reason to suppose that some step forward in the history of human salvation has been secured. Conversely, if they are not archetypes for all humanity, anything they may have accomplished is an accomplishment for them alone. Only if both conditions are satisfied can we speak of sacred history, the discovery of perpetual meaning in actual people and events.

But why pick on these exemplars? For Augustine the primacy of Scripture is certain: "[T]here is no untruth of any kind in the Scripture, whose reliability in the account of past events is attested by the fulfilment of its prophecies for the future . . ." (*City of God*, Book XVI, Chap. 9). There is good reason to doubt the logic of this line of argument. It is like supposing that the skill of the punter in predicting future winners is confirmation of his account of races far in the past, whereas the two abilities—predicting and recording—are quite distinct. But the more interesting question for present purposes is whether, assuming their historicity, individuals can constitute 'types' which, under scrutiny, can be made to reveal perpetual meaning or significance for all who occupy the human condition. The ability to do so is an essential part of the whole enterprise. And indeed, the plausibility of almost all sacred histories rests upon the possibility of finding exemplars through whom the continuity of the story is preserved.

One question which naturally arises is this. What constrains the interpretation of historical figures or events as exemplars? In his interpretation of the Bible Augustine is given to a good deal of numerology and philology which cannot but strike us as contrived and fanciful, and in some cases simply mistaken. (He is flatly wrong about the meaning of the name 'Babylon', for instance, confusing 'balal' with 'Babil'.) To say this is not to diminish his achievement. Augustine was in most respects self-taught, and in many ways the ideas he was struggling with were such that there was little previous reflection he could call upon. Moreover, it does not follow from the fancifulness of some of his reasoning that his attempt to find symbolic meaning in biblical figures is mistaken. On this score he advances an argument which has some substance.

Surely it is only a twisted mind that would maintain that books which have been so scrupulously preserved for thousands of years, which have been safeguarded by such a concern for such a well ordered transmission, that such books were written without serious purpose, or that we should consult them simply for historical facts. (*City of God*, Book XV, Chap. 27)

That many of the books of the Bible purport to be accounts of the past is incontestable, but they are not all of this nature. The Book of Job or the Psalms, for instance, though not wholly without historical overtones, are largely works of spiritual meditation and reflection. The preservation and transmission of these Scriptures, consequently, cannot be understood simply as the maintenance of historical records. Furthermore, the many millions of human beings who have searched them, have done so with a view to finding meaning or significance both in their own lives, and in human experience as a whole, and in so doing they have attached importance not only to the more spiritual books, but to the historical books also. To dismiss this as simple error is, at the least, to run the risk of failing to uncover important possibilities for human thought, and Augustine thought this so obvious he could only describe the mind which persisted in dismissing them as twisted.

This defence of the Scriptures as a source of sacred history, however, does not secure them against misconception. Still less does it solve the philosophical and conceptual problems which Augustine's conceptions of epochs, exemplars and the like encounter. We still need to know how it is possible for the historical and the symbolic to be united, and how, out of the full range of the historical, the symbolically significant is to be detected. Here again Augustine himself makes use of reasoning which contemporary minds are unlikely to find persuasive. The various 'ages', for instance, are differentiated often by close scrutiny of the mathematics employed or implied in those long genealogies which modern Bible lectionaries almost always omit. So to make much headway with the question it is necessary to find methods other than Augustine's and start thinking afresh. This does not, as we shall see, mean the abandonment of his conception of sacred history, to which we will return in Section VII.

III

One way of proceeding is to look at the concept of a miracle. This has a number of advantages. First, miracles play an important role in the Bible, both Old and New Testaments. Second, miracles have the double nature in which we are interested. To be convincing of anything they must actually have happened, but declaring them miracles attributes to them a far greater significance than ordinary events. Third, the concept of miracle has been extensively discussed in analytical philosophy, so that by beginning with miracles we use philosophical methods to tackle larger issues less frequently discussed by philosophers.

David Hume (1711–76), in his famous sceptical essay *On Miracles* argues that the very idea of a miracle carries the implication that we can never have good reason to suppose one to have happened. The precise interpretation to be given to his argument is a matter of some debate, but one version is this. Since a miracle is an event contrary to a law of nature, and since a law of nature is a record of uniform experience, should any one tell us of a miracle's occurring, we always have more reason to suppose that the person who reports the miracle is lying, deceived or mistaken, than we have to believe that it actually happened.

Critics of Hume have argued that by his account a reputed law of nature could never be shown to be false, since we would never have reason to believe anyone who claimed to have witnessed its failure. Others have pointed out that he fails to undermine first-person evidence that a miracle has occurred. If the laws of nature are ultimately based on sense experience, which Hume as a good empiricist must agree, my own sense experience must be more authoritative than any law-like generalization derived from it. But more important for present purposes is a third line of criticism, that Hume's identification of miracles with violations of laws of nature locates their significance in the wrong place.

Consider two examples. It is well attested that salt dissolves in water. Suppose I put some salt in water and it fails to dissolve. Further testing demonstrates that the two substances are indeed ordinary water and ordinary salt. The phenomenon is certainly puzzling and might call for some serious scientific rethinking, but there is nothing in the event so described that would give us reason to think we had encountered the miraculous. Conversely, take the 'Pool of Siloam' miracle in the New Testament (John 9). Jesus is recorded as meeting a blind man who asks for his sight to be restored. Spitting on the ground, Jesus makes a paste which he puts on the man's eyes, murmuring a few words. The man is told to wash off the mud in the Pool of Siloam and when he does so, he can see. What is there here that is contrary to any known law of nature? Scarcely a month passes without a newspaper report of sight being mysteriously restored. Such events, of course, despite being *familiar*, are none the less relatively *rare*. They are also difficult to explain in standard physiological ways. But their rarity, and their inexplicability, do not result from their being contrary to laws of nature conceived upon Humean lines.

What these two examples show is that Hume is mistaken in supposing it to be a defining characteristic of miracles that they are events contrary to laws of nature. Violation of a law of nature is neither a sufficient nor a necessary condition of something's being declared miraculous. What the first example lacks is any context of human or divine significance, while in the second example, the concern of the Gospel writer and the participants, both for and against Jesus, is not only whether the event really happened, but how it relates to sinfulness. As in several other instances, where Jesus' own explanation of healing is that "your faith has made you whole", what matters primarily is how this event is to be interpreted theologically, as indicative of the sinfulness of the man and/or the sinlessness of Jesus. The application of religious conceptions is thus at the heart of the identification of the miracle. It is not that something highly unusual happens, and from this we are to infer the action of God, but rather that having believed, or not believed, in the power of God over all things, we find it instanced in the unusual.

Hume is certainly right, in my view, that religious belief is often surrounded by unsubstantiated claims about fantastical doings and events, and he is probably correct in the animating belief of his *Natural History of Religion* that there is almost no limit to the superstitiousness of human beings. Nevertheless the analysis of miracles just offered is consonant with at least one way in which they are commonly conceived. The parents who pray that their ailing child may survive against the odds believe in a connection between the prayer and the outcome such that the child's survival is not merely something devoutly wished for, but a desire to be granted. It is this that gives thankfulness a focus, and hence a meaning. While it is true that people without religious belief not infrequently express thankfulness for good outcomes, this is, arguably, an expression without meaning. Whom are they thanking? To raise this doubt is not to deny that the non-religious can experience great depths of emotion, profound feelings of relief and happiness. But it is to question the meaningfulness of expressing these feelings in the language of thanks, and to imply that at best such language is parasitical upon other ways of thinking. Without the presupposition of some superhuman agency, there is in fact no meaningful distinction to be drawn between gratitude and relief.

IV

One line of thought which emerges from these reflections is this. It is a fact about human beings that they find themselves caught up in what we might call a dialectic between the events of their lives on the one hand, and the emotions they experience on the other, such that they cannot but invoke and test varying interpretations of that experience in terms of their adequacy to the emotions. This is the phenomenon, I think, that is being pointed to when human beings are said to be 'incurably religious'. Religious belief is generated by the need to make intellect and emotion cohere. Its peculiarly religious character, however, comes more plainly to the fore when the emotions evoked by experience are those not so much prompted by or focused on the local events of individual lives (as in the parent and child example), though these are of considerable importance, but generalized, universalistic emotions—a sense of pervading worthlessness, a consuming psychological elation, an intimation of the transcendent, a keen perception of mortality. These more distinctively religious emotions are specially marked in some people, the greatest of whom attain the status of saints and prophets. One such was John Bunyan. In his writings Bunyan reveals a power of religious emotion that has few equals. Something of the flavour of his sense of being under judgement, for example, may be caught in these few sentences from *Grace Abounding to the Chief of Sinners*.

I was much followed by this scripture, "Simon, Simon, behold Satan hath desired to *have* you". And sometimes it would sound so loud within me and as it were call so strongly after me, that once above all the rest, I turned my head over my shoulder, thinking verily some man had, behind me, called to me. (Bunyan, pp. 30–1)

Though Bunyan's is a specially remarkable case, it is only one among thousands, all of them merely striking examples of a much more widespread, and recurring, human tendency. It is a tendency in which Augustine shared more than most. To understand his sacred history we have to understand that it is formed out of a dialectic between religious emotion, biblical narratives, and contemporary events. This dialectical structure is shared by almost every similar sacred history. The prophet Jeremiah, in common with his contemporaries, was both struck and distressed by the disasters befalling Judaea; given their catastrophic nature it would have been difficult for the inhabitants of Judaea not to be. He thus found himself in the standard situation in which people ask themselves 'What does it all mean?' Setting these catastrophes alongside both the wickedness of the ruling classes and the religious fecklessness of the people, his inherited belief in a covenant with Yahweh, and his own intense religious feeling, Jeremiah forged a ready explanation. The disasters were divine chastisements for wickedness, to be averted only by a return to national life conducted within the terms of a new covenant with Yahweh. It is out of all these elements, and not merely the abstract desire to record the past and explain contemporary events, that his sacred history emerges.

It would be wrong to conclude from this, however, that sacred history is essentially 'projectivist', that it consists in the projection of feeling and desire on to the perceived events of the past. Jeremiah, Augustine, and Bunyan, in company with every other major religious figure, thought themselves to be grappling not merely with emotion but with realities—the real cause of national disaster, the real meaning of history, a real battle with satanic power. If the emotional engine of sacred history is ineliminable, so too is the intellectual effort to give it shape and coherence. This is the point of describing all such endeavours as a dialectic between emotion and understanding. This brings us back to an earlier problem—the relation between the two elements, historical and symbolic, upon both of which Augustine insists—and allows us now to say something about it. In sacred history, historical and symbolic attitudes are combined. The historical attitude seeks to establish what has happened or is happening, the symbolic seeks to place upon it an interpretation adequate to its human, emotional significance. The relationship is dialectical, for as in the Pharisees' questioning of the healing of the blind man, theological doubts can raise doubts about what actually happened, and vice versa.

But to say that the two elements are combined is to say that in this dialectic there must be a serious concern with how the past really was. What part, then, do evidence and the like play in constraining sacred history? By what criteria are the significant and the insignificant to be distinguished?

In trying to answer these questions, it is worth repeating that sacred history has two important features—it is narrative in structure and the narrative relates the actions and purposes of an intentional agent, God. This narrative structure makes it possible to begin by considering the conceptual nature of other intentional narratives, namely those composed by human beings. It has sometimes been thought that an illuminating parallel to be drawn here is one between sacred history and a work of creative fiction, say a play or a novel. Thus, God has not infrequently been referred to as the *author* of history. But whatever initial plausibility this parallel may have, it is not in fact a very promising line of inquiry, because from the outset there appears to be a clear and important disanalogy between the two. God is not merely the author of sacred history but an active agent in it. The playwright, by contrast, is not a character in his own play. This is why a better analogy is to be found between sacred history and large-scale human endeavours, a battle, an expedition, a campaign of espionage, or the building of a city for instance, in which the actions of many different individuals are under the direction of a controlling mind, that of the general, explorer, or spymaster, but where that mind, though not directly engaged in fighting or exploring or building, does itself play an active part and does not merely write out instructions.

V

Any of these examples provides an analogy more promising than that of a play, but it is the parallel with armies in battle that I propose to investigate further. To soldiers on the battlefield at least two things are often obscure—the strategy of the battle as a whole, and the purpose and policy of the war of which this battle is a part. We and they can construe their task as playing their part to good effect, not merely as instruments but as deliberating agents. A self-conscious ability to do so, which is to say an understanding of the role which they can arrive at and recognize to be meaningful, depends crucially both upon their correctly identifying the part they are to play and upon this part being an element in a larger whole which is itself effectively purposeful. The attitude, memorably captured forever by Tennyson— "theirs not to reason why, theirs but to do and die"—may have something admirable about it, and it may also be useful to those in command of armies. But the fact remains that on its own, as in the actual charge of the Light Brigade which prompted Tennyson's poem, it can result in nothing more than pointless, wasted self-destruction. The exaltation of blind obedience, which is a familiar feature of attitudes to war together with the praise which the spirit it betokens frequently elicits, are perhaps attributable to the fact that pointless destruction in war is a lamentably common occurrence with which many people have had to come to terms. The Crimean War in which the charge of the Light Brigade took place is one such instance, the American Civil War another. In both, for want of adequate generalship, especially on the Union side in the Civil War, hundreds of thousands died. Not infrequently they did so in conditions which called forth almost superhuman courage and endurance. Yet the truth is that their doing so served no purpose, and the loss of life, despite so much heroic virtue, was simple waste.[1]

So, if the common soldier is not to be a mere instrument of blind obedience but to see value in what he does, and especially if he is to make sense of deep feelings of courage and commitment, he needs to understand his activity on the field by placing it in a larger context. In doing so, he has to take some view of events of which he is not the author, but simply one participating agent. He must, consequently, make an attempt to discern tactics, strategies, and policies emanating from minds at ever greater distances from his own. For such a soldier, it would, except in special cases, be absurd to think the High Command has special tasks for *him*. Nevertheless, there is a plain sense in which his actions can either be part of an intended plan, or run outside or against it. It follows that the feelings and attitudes that accompany his actions will be well or badly placed in so far as they accord with a true understanding of the whole. People can be foolishly mistaken about the importance of their contributions to a war effort, and they can also be mistakenly sceptical about their worth.

An essential part of this understanding consists in making certain distinctions. First, it is necessary for a soldier to distinguish actions relevant to his role as a soldier from those that are merely the coincidental actions of living. Second, among the relevant actions, it is necessary to distinguish degrees of importance. To treat everything he needs to do or is required to do as either equally important or equally trivial is mistaken, whatever his feelings about them, in so far as it is out of keeping with their

---

[1] The classic historical account of the charge of the Light Brigade is Cecil Woodham Smith, *The Reason Why* (Constable, London, 1953). Of the very many accounts of the American Civil War, one of the most recent and best is James M. McPherson, *Battle Cry of Freedom*.

actual place in the larger plan. This possibility is of great significance to his self-understanding, for to bring deep-seated feeling to bear on the wrong things, is to render the effort he puts into them a mockery. At many points and on many occasions, of course, the common soldier must trust to faith. That the actions to which he attaches great importance and of which he is proud do indeed form part of an effective tactic within a sensible strategy to a good end may be more than he can know. Perhaps the most he can reasonably hope for is not to know to the contrary. But this only shows how precarious is the attempt to make sense of our lives, and how understandable is the inclination just to live for the moment instead.

VI

It is not hard to see how the analogy with sacred history is to be drawn. The same dialectic between emotion, belief, understanding, and faith is to be found there too. But precisely because the parallels are easy to see, it is more instructive to consider the disanalogies. Some of these may be unimportant. For instance, both Jews and Christians who believe themselves to be part of God's providential action in history quite commonly claim to be the recipients of 'particular' as well as 'general' revelation. They thereby suppose that God commissions 'front line' individuals directly in a way that military commanders do not. But though not without interest, this difference is a matter of detail. Other disanalogies are more compelling.

The overall context to which soldiers must relate their actions and activity, if it is to have meaning and value, is one formed by goals and aspirations somewhat beyond their ken. The international or economic aims of political leaders and the campaign strategies of field marshals are likely to require a knowledge and vision greater than the average footsoldier can in the normal course of things be expected to comprehend (though of course there may be many exceptions to this generalization). Nevertheless, there is *some* general description of these which will make sense to him. Such aims as victory over enemies, defence of a homeland and its people, conquest of valuable territory, or greater security within a balance of power, are all goals whose value is pretty much evident to any human being. It may not be true, certainly, that whenever these are revealed, they will command the support of all those who are obliged to fight for them; soldiers need not share or even approve of the objects for which they are obliged to fight. But they are at least intelligible as goals, and can be distinguished by almost anyone from intrinsically pointless or simply lunatic military aims. Such was the aim of the mad emperor Caligula, who sought to prove his own divinity by having his soldiers fill chests with sea shells, and declared it to be the seizure of Neptune's treasure. To this extent the minds of emperors and princes, however large and lofty, cannot be wholly removed from those of their lowliest servants, and because this is so, the hope of making sense of activity at any and every level of a large-scale human endeavour is a reasonable one. But can the same be said about the religious case? The mind of God, we may reasonably suppose, far surpasses that of humankind. What reason is there, then, to think that even if we could discern the divine purpose of history, this would make sense of *our* lives?

A second disanalogy is related to this. The significance of a war, and the place of individuals in it, however vast and all-consuming an enterprise it might be, resides ultimately in values derived from a wider context than that of the war itself—happiness and prosperity, moral principle, the achievement of ambition, the exercise of power, the maintenance of peace, the protection of culture. All these are recurrent features of human existence *per se*, and not merely of this or that war or scheme of advancement. By contrast, the aspiration of religion, and hence the aspiration of sacred history, is in part to derive all these, and any other, values from some transcendental source whose value and significance is not itself explained in this way. But is this not to seek, incoherently, for an explanation of everything? Explanations, it has been remarked, must come to an end somewhere. If so, it follows that the thing on which the last step in the explanation rests cannot itself be explained, hence the impossibility of an explanation of everything. If this is indeed what religion and sacred history seeks, its basic aspiration is incoherent and thus unattainable.

A third important disanalogy is somewhat different to the first two. In his attempt to make sense of his activities, to give them meaning and value in the overall scheme of things, the soldier must have recourse to information. This includes what he gleans from newspapers and radio, if such he has, his own experience of events, the reports of his fellow soldiers, the orders of his officers, and what he can infer from all these. It is possible, of course, and may sometimes have happened (the First World War is perhaps an example), that the whole world in which he moves is caught in a massive delusion and that consequently all the beliefs, actions and utterances on which he relies are deeply at odds with reality. Still, in assessing the evidence at his disposal, the ordinary soldier can rely on many of the normal checking procedures learned in everyday life and practised in relation to the limited facts of immediate existence. He has the use of his own eyes on the battlefield, and his belief in the power and authority of the command structure, for instance, can be tested against its ability to supply him with food and shelter.

When we move to the parallel with religion, however, the relevance and availability of these procedures are much less certain. Since the purposes of God are not to be discerned directly through the senses, and since those who purport to know of them speak in non-standard ways and not infrequently are bearers of mixed messages, the possibilities for 'checking' are limited, or themselves require a special insight which not everyone will have. By and large the authenticity and authority of officers in an army is easily ascertained in a way that the authenticity and authority of prophetic voices is not, and though it is true that what one can see for oneself is often insufficient to establish whether the outcome of a battle, still less a war, is success or failure, this is different to the ways in which personal experience is insufficient to establish the reality of divine intervention.

Can we sustain the parallel between the narratives of sacred history and the narratives of large-scale human projects in the face of these disanalogies? There are at least some replies to be attempted. Consider first the difference between the purposes of God and those of human beings. This does not seem an insurmountable obstacle provided there is a measure of continuity between the two. In fact, there is no great dissimilarity here, since in many contexts the aspirations of individuals at one level of activity may be seen to surpass those of individuals on a lower level, while at the same time being continuous with them. The child learning to talk is set upon a trajectory whose culmination, if it makes sense to speak of such a thing in this context, exceeds anything that he or she can conceive. The power and potentiality of language is so very great that it allows for thought and articulation far beyond that which most people can attain. The average speaker of German has relatively little prospect of understanding Kant, but there is none the less a continuity of language and thought linking one to the other. In like fashion, we may imagine that the purposes of God, though for the most part beyond our understanding, are not radically dissimilar but only further along a spectrum on which our own are formed. Such a supposition, it is true, relies on the idea that God too is a person, or conversely that human beings are made in the image of God, but this is a fundamental presupposition of the Jewish and Christian religions, and may thus be granted to the proponents of their sacred histories.

The second disanalogy can be dealt with in something of the same fashion, though the topic is so large that its resolution can only be gestured at here. The pursuit of a meaningful life on the part of human beings is an effort to find an interpretation of existence that bestows upon it both value and intelligibility. If my analysis in terms of a dialectic is correct, this pursuit is to be construed as an attempt to find a satisfactory match between the beliefs we form and the emotions we have. Such a match is found, for example, when pride and satisfaction are focused upon something truly worthwhile. The nature of the pursuit, however, is such as to seek ever widening interpretative contexts, and in this sense to transcend limitations of belief and feeling. Some of these limitations are a consequence of poor forms of inquiry or narrowness of mind and spirit. But some, or so human beings repeatedly believe, are limitations set by the nature of temporal humanity itself. There is a strong human tendency, as Wittgenstein put it, "to run up against the bars of our cage". Whether this tendency is senseless or profound is not altogether to the point. What satisfies it, if anything does, is the postulation of a higher frame of reference, an "enduring power, not ourselves, that works for righteousness", as Matthew Arnold (1822–88) famously expressed it in *Literature and Dogma*. In the same place Arnold describes God as "simply the stream of tendency by which all things seek to fulfil the law of their being" and in so far as the law of our being, as intelligent agents, is to seek ever larger interpretations, it does indeed lead to religious ideas and conceptions. These conceptions, by their nature, give rise to thoughts and expressions which are perplexingly paradoxical. Whether they indicate the mystical or the nonsensical is a vexed question because the line between mystery and mumbo-jumbo is very hard to determine, and not a matter to be settled here.[2] But the recurrent nature of this tendency of the human mind at least gives us reason to hesitate over accepting too quickly the conclusion of the simple

[2] I have addressed some of the relevant issues in 'Mystery and Mumbo-jumbo', *Philosophical Investigations*, 1984.

logical argument about explanation on which the second disanalogy rests, for if we are not to dismiss such a pervasive human tendency outright, we must allow that the suppositions upon which it rests may themselves stand in need of revision. To conclude in this way, of course, is only to say that while the sort of aspiration we find in sacred history does indeed pass beyond the range of human values, there is reason to resist the suggestion that it has thereby passed beyond the humanly valuable.

The third disanalogy is, as it seems to me, more troublesome to the idea of sacred history. It may be summarized as the disanalogy between the authority of normal knowledge and the authority of prophetic insight. Returning to the case of the soldier in battle we can say that any mundane understanding he has of his circumstances, however difficult to achieve, rests on nothing more unusual than the normal procedures of experience, induction and deduction. To pass from this to the more ambitious understanding which sacred history aims to supply requires the acceptance of prophetic insight and supernatural authority. In Chapter 4 I argued that appeal to the supernatural, properly conceived, is inescapable for human will and understanding. Nevertheless there is a special difficulty here. The world seems to be embarrassingly rich in claimants to religious truth. Even if we have no doubts about the possibility of spiritual revelation, we might still be uncertain as to where, amongst all the contenders, it is actually to be found.

VII

This brings us back, in fact, to a question raised in the early part of this chapter, the authority of Scripture. On this question, as we saw, Augustine has no doubts—"there is no untruth of any kind in the Scripture". But for those who are less certain it is reasonable to ask for the basis upon which we are to believe this.

The Bible itself has answers. The trouble is that they are all, so to speak, internal. Thus, the 'proof' in the Gospel of Matthew that Jesus is the Messiah is given as the fact that his life is the fulfilment of the law and the prophets. But to accept this as a reason is to presuppose both the authority of the Old Testament and the accuracy of the New, which is just what is being questioned. Again, when Jesus, in the Gospel of John is asked "Tell us plainly: are you the Messiah?", he replies "My deeds done in my Father's name are my credentials but because you are not sheep of my flock you do not believe" (10: 26). If we are on the inside, so to speak, we have proof which, being on the inside we do not need, and if we are on the outside, where we do need it, it is lacking. The same sort of move is found in what is probably the earliest form of the new Christian Gospel, the kerygma in Chap 2 of the Acts of the Apostles. Here Peter rests his case for the attribution of divinity to Christ on three things: his fulfilment of the prophets, the miracles he performed, and most importantly, his having been raised from the dead and appearing to many. But again, we can only be reasonably persuaded of this if we accept the authority of the very thing whose authority is in question. The reasoning in all these instances turns in the circle described (unintentionally no doubt) by St Paul in the Epistle to the Romans.

Scripture says . . . 'Everyone who calls on the name of the Lord will be saved'. But how could they call on him without having faith in him? And how could they have heard without someone to spread the news? And how could anyone spread the news without being sent? . . . So then faith does come through hearing, and hearing through the word of Christ. (10: 11–17)

What we have here is what Alasdair MacIntyre calls "a Christian version of the paradox of Plato's *Meno*: it seems that only by learning what texts have to teach can [the reader] come to read those texts aright, but also that only by reading them aright can he or she learn what the texts have to teach" (MacIntyre, *Three*

Rival Versions, p. 82). But how is such a circle to be broken into?

The answer many Christians have given, following St Paul, is 'personal experience of the Risen Lord'. Paul's belief in Christ as God incarnate began, not in personal acquaintance with the historical Jesus, but with his dramatic, religious, conversion on the road to Damascus. Those who have not undergone this sort of experience will not be any better off with this answer, of course. But even those who think they have had experience of this kind may still encounter a logical difficulty. How are they to know that the 'Christ' of their experience is to be identified with the Christ of the Scriptures?

The only further step to be taken in the face of this difficulty, I think, is to widen what has been called 'the hermeneutic circle'. Appropriately, the term 'hermeneutics' originally referred to exegesis of the Scriptures, though it has since come to refer to any exegetical endeavour which interprets by locating phenomena in an ever larger context—linguistic, literary, social, and cultural. In the case we are concerned with here, this circle must take in sacred texts and their interpretation, first person and third person religious experience, and, crucially, the tradition of devotional practice and intellectual inquiry in which the relation between the two has been elaborated and refined. 'Widening the circle' means attempting to fashion into a coherent whole, personal spiritual experience, putative prophetic utterance, factual belief, and common understanding. But it also means doing so in the context of a tradition of religious and intellectual practices of inquiry with their own history.

This last element is of great importance. It is what makes the technique of widening the circle crucially different from the approach to Scripture, religious belief and sacred history found among those the seventeenth century called 'sectaries'. These groups, composed of Protestants and freethinkers, believed that each individual must take his or her own mind to be authoritative.

In the case of Protestantism this meant primarily that individuals must read and interpret the Scriptures for themselves. In a wider context it meant the rejection of traditional cultural and social authorities, which is one reason why the sectaries were largely regarded by the traditional ruling classes as dangerous radicals who comprised, in Bunyan's phrase "a turbulent, seditious and factious people".

The causes of this radical individualism, which encourages complete reliance on personal experience and judgement, lie in a powerful historical combination of the Protestant Reformation, a revolt against the corrupt dogmatism of the Church, and the emergence of a highly successful scientific empiricism at the hands of, among others, Francis Bacon (1561–1626) which advanced so rapidly in the late sixteenth century. Its effect on Western culture has been immense, and for this reason difficult to escape. But arguably it is only against a background assumption of what might be called epistemological individualism that radical scepticism about sacred history, and the idea of moral and religious knowledge it employs, is plausible. Once this 'sectarian' assumption is questioned, the third disanalogy which we are here examining becomes much less marked.

And in fact, there does seem to be something contradictory at work in Baconian individualism. Even the most ardent Protestant sectaries in the seventeenth century looked to the Bible for authoritative guidance, and generally held, no less than Augustine, that there was no untruth anywhere in it. Indeed it was the authority they lent to Holy Writ which led them to attack the liberal Latitudinarians so vigorously. What they themselves rejected was the authority of the tradition of inquiry and interpretation which had grown up around it. In short, they rejected *orthodoxy* in scriptural interpretation and ecclesiastical order. But in doing so they abandoned the only defence they might have had against a more radical scepticism still, that of the Ranters, Quakers, Anabaptists, and atheists against whom they also found themselves ranged. There was much to be said in favour of the reformers' protest against the corrupt clericalism of the Church, and hence something to be said for the increasingly popular doctrine of 'the priesthood of all believers', but once the further move was made according to which each individual became an interpretative law unto himself, the reformers lost any authority for the interpretations they believed to be preferable. The idea of a hermeneutic 'widening of the circle' is in effect an attempt to restore the role and authority of tradition.

Amongst contemporary philosophers, it is MacIntyre who has laid greatest emphasis on the deep incoherence of radical individualism and the corresponding strength of traditions of inquiry as the foundation of rational belief. In his 1988 Gifford Lectures, subsequently published under the title *Three Versions of Moral Inquiry* he continues his longstanding project of overcoming the moral collapse identified in *After Virtue*. But without returning to the issues examined in Chapter 5, we can usefully call upon his point about tradition in the present context. The sectary is someone who believes that the interpretation of experience, and of religion in particular, can, so to speak, begin *de novo*. Yet, in the very act of pursuing an interpretation by which he may better understand his existence, he is set upon a path of inquiry which can only make sense if it employs canons of inquiry which he has not himself invented but inherited. All such canons, however, are historical products, and it is a mistake to suppose that any understanding can be achieved in rejection or in ignorance of that history.

[B]ecause at any particular moment the rationality of a craft is justified by its history so far, which has made it what it is in that specific time, place, and set of historical circumstances, such rationality is inseparable from the tradition through which it was achieved. To share in the rationality of a craft requires sharing in the contingencies of its history, understanding its story as one's own, and finding a place for oneself as a character in the enacted dramatic narrative which is that story so far. (MacIntyre, *Three Rival Versions*, p. 65)

Moreover, at the heart of such a tradition is the master/apprentice relationship. The sectary is like a would-be carpenter who supposes that he could begin to make furniture in ignorance of inherited ends and methods. In the 'craft' of rational understanding, no less than in manual crafts, our only choice is to begin where we find ourselves and hence to accept both the authority of what has gone before and of those who have already mastered it.

The authority of a master is both more and other than a matter of exemplifying the best standards so far. It is also and most importantly a matter of knowing how to go further and especially how to direct others towards going further, using what can be learned from the tradition afforded by the past to move towards the *telos* of fully perfected work. It is thus in knowing how to link past and future that those with authority are able to draw upon tradition, to interpret and reinterpret it, so that its directedness towards the *telos* of that particular craft becomes apparent in new and characteristically unexpected ways. And it is the ability to teach others how to learn this type of knowing how that the power of the master within the community of a craft is legitimated as rational authority. (*Three Rival Versions*, pp. 65–6)

MacIntyre draws heavily upon the epistemological presuppositions of Augustinian theology, and it is partly this that makes his exploration of these issues specially relevant to sacred history. Those who set out in search of an understanding of their experience must engage in information gathering. The disanalogy between a soldier who attempts to understand the war of which he is a tiny part, and the person who seeks to understand his place in the history of salvation, was said to be the relative certainty which his own fact finding has for the former, in contrast to the bewildering cacophony of prophetic voices which besiege the latter. But from the point of view of Augustinian theology, and there is reason to think it is right on this point, there are at least two mistakes in this way of construing matters. The 'certainty' of the personal, empirical method is an illusion. Here, as elsewhere, investigation and interpretation, if they are to accomplish anything, must employ standards of rationality which necessarily go beyond anything individuals could secure for themselves. There may be a difference in the complexity of the kinds of understanding sought, but there is no deep logical difference. Second, even in the case of religion there are methods of sifting and sorting waiting to be employed which traditions of inquiry and interpretation have formed and made authoritative. This is the force in Augustine's argument that it is wrong to think that "books which have been so scrupulously preserved for thousands of years, which have been safeguarded by such a concern for such a well ordered transmission, that such books were written without serious purpose, or that we should consult them simply for historical facts" (*City of God*, Book XV, Chap. 27).

Augustine, as we saw, was led by this argument to assert rather baldly that "there is no untruth anywhere" in the Scriptures. No doubt this is to go too far. But the more qualified claim that the traditional canon and the traditional interpretation which surrounds it have rational authority is more plausible, for that tradition is the outcome of human experience and genius. If Christian sacred history in the Augustinian mould holds, therefore, that this larger body of material is an authoritative basis upon which to build a religious interpretation of the past, its claim has considerable substance.

VIII

But there is more to it than this. By Augustine's account, induction and participation in a tradition launches the inquirer upon an activity in which there is just that dialectic between the individual and the object of his or her understanding which was described earlier. As MacIntyre puts it:

The intellect and the desires do not naturally move towards that good which is at once the foundation for knowledge and that from which lesser goods flow. The will which directs them is initially perverse and needs a kind of redirection which will enable it to trust obediently in a teacher who will guide the mind towards the discovery both of its own resources and of what lies outside the mind, both in nature and in God. Hence faith in authority has to precede rational understanding. And hence the acquisition of that virtue which the will requires to be guided, humility, is the necessary first step in education or in self-education. In learning therefore we move towards and not from first principles and we discover truth only insofar as we discover the conformity of particulars to the forms in relation to which those particulars become intelligible, a relationship apprehended only by the mind illuminated by God. (*Three Rival Versions*, p. 84)

It is in this way that the attempt to understand experience leads on to sacred history.

This technique of 'widening the circle' by appeal to tradition, however, still has its difficulties. It may diminish the cacophony of discordant voices, but it does not eliminate it completely since there exist rival traditions. The existence of these rivals is in fact the principal subject of MacIntyre's lectures, as their title indicates. It is a matter of some dispute and considerable difficulty whether his line of thought, even if it answers the challenge of radical scepticism, does not in the end imply a kind of relativism. In other words, between the competing claims of rival traditions of inquiry of sufficient sophistication there can be no ultimate resolution.

There are several contexts in which this possibility raises great difficulties. Were it to be the case in natural science, for instance, the metaphysics of realism upon which the intelligibility of science seems to rest would be called in question. It is belief in a radical relativism in science that leads the American philosopher

Paul Feyerabend, in his book *Against Method*, to a belief in a scientific anarchism according to which the history of scientific theory is the outcome of social and cultural forces rather than rational progress. But how great a threat is the possibility of relativism in the present context? Perhaps the sort of understanding sacred history seeks, its *telos*, does not require exclusivity in its answers. Or better, perhaps its *telos* is such that it can be satisfied with something less than this. A clue to this issue may be found in the language MacIntyre uses to describe the aims of the rational inquirer in the passage quoted earlier. "To share in the rationality of a craft requires sharing in the contingencies of its history, understanding its story as one's own, and finding a place for oneself as a character in the enacted dramatic narrative which is that story so far" (*Three Rival Versions*, p. 65).

MacIntyre means to argue for a quite general account of rational inquiry, but this passage is, to say the least, an odd way of describing the activity of the inquiring scientist, since science aims, it is more natural to think, at a view of the world in which personal desires and practical interest play no part. But it is a rather better description of the soldier in battle with whom an extended analogy has been drawn, and an even more plausible description of the aim of sacred history. Indeed, it is here, I think, that we discover the peculiarity of sacred history and of philosophical history more generally: its desire to combine objective historical understanding with 'finding a place for oneself' in the narrative, of making a home out of history. The exploration of this idea, in fact, will provide a useful context for drawing together the threads of the previous chapters in a concluding one.

8 The Practical Past

THE preceding chapters have examined almost all the ways in which people have thought about history, but there is one further attitude which has not as yet been expressly discussed. A distinction has been drawn between the desire to have a knowledge of the past entirely for its own sake and a more practical attitude which aims to uncover hidden meanings of relevance to the conduct of life. The 'hidden' character of these meanings is specially marked in sacred history, but another less esoteric, more practical view of the past conceives of it as a valuable repository of recoverable lessons for present and future action.

The idea that humanity might learn from its mistakes and successes in the way that an individual does has had distinguished adherents. The most famous of these is probably the sixteenth-century Italian political theorist Machiavelli, though there have been many others, notably Henry St John, 1st Viscount Bolingbroke, the English politician and political thinker (1678–1761). Both Machiavelli and Bolingbroke wrote handbooks for princes, and in assembling their advice both drew upon history. Bolingbroke is less obviously a collector of historical lessons. In one of his books, *On the Study and Use of History*, he repeats with approval the dictum that "History is Philosophy teaching by examples" (Letter 2), though his best known work, *The Idea of a Patriot King*, whose aim is rather to outline the constitution and character of the ideal ruler, makes use of history more by way of illustration than in the application of principles of conduct systematically gathered from the experience of the past. Elizabeth I is his primary model. He also illustrates many of his points by reference to Alexander the Great, Julius Caesar, and Mark Antony. But his appeal to these exemplars does not really consist in the formulation of a set of principles of political conduct systematically rooted in history.

In this he is to be contrasted with Machiavelli (1469–1527) whose most famous book, *The Prince*, had appeared over 200 years earlier. *The Prince* is much more obviously a set of guides to action for the ruler. On page after page general principles are enunciated, explained, and defended on the grounds of historical precedents. The opening of Chapter VII is typical:

Those who rise from private citizens to be princes merely by fortune have little trouble in rising but very much in maintaining their position . . . the first storm destroys them, unless . . . the man who thus becomes a prince is of such great genius as to be able to take steps for maintaining what fortune has thrown into his lap . . . With regard to these two methods of becoming a prince—by ability or by good fortune, I will here adduce two examples . . .

And so the whole book proceeds. In another, larger work, generally regarded as his masterpiece, Machiavelli takes the same approach. The *Discourses on the First Decade of Titus Livius* is somewhat misnamed, since it is not specially concerned with Livy and where it is, it does not restrict itself to his first decade. Like *The Prince*, it comprises sets of general principles of political conduct exemplified by historical examples. It also contains what is perhaps his plainest explanation and endorsement of the 'practical historical' method.

What is the science of medicine but the experience of ancient physicians, which their successors have taken as their guide . . . [t]he majority . . . [never] think of imitating the noble actions, deeming that not only difficult but impossible; as though heaven, the sun, the elements, and men had changed the order of their motions and powers, and were different from what they were in ancient times. (*Discourses*, pp. 104–5)

But if drawing general principles for past occasions is Machiavelli's express method, he is not very good at using it. Sydney Anglo, discussing the point says: "This is supposed to be Machiavelli's new method, his 'untrodden path'. He says so himself frequently. But it was not new: his own use of the technique was not methodical; and, properly speaking, it does not constitute Machiavelli's method at all" (*Machiavelli*, pp. 216–17).

In defence of his first contention Anglo goes on to note that the idea of using history as a fund of material from which to draw forth supposedly practical lessons was common throughout the Middle Ages and the Renaissance, and was indeed already archaic by Machiavelli's time. But the originality or consistency of Machiavelli is not of great moment here. *The Prince* and *The Idea of a Patriot King* constitute two famous examples of a recurrent way of thinking about the past, namely one which takes it to be of practical relevance. The influence of both books, especially *The Prince*, on politicians and political theorists has been greatly exaggerated, but they have been influential in keeping alive an idea of practical history which, while more common in the Middle Ages and the Renaissance, has continued to have its enthusiasts.

I

In most versions, this practical attitude to history finds value chiefly in its application to politics, though there is no reason in principle why it should not be extended more widely to other aspects of culture. But whether restricted to politics or not, its logical structure is the same, namely inductive generalization. By surveying the facts of the past, its proponents hope to arrive at valid general rules which can usefully be applied to present and future cases. This is certainly what Machiavelli *aims* to do, as the chapter titles of the *Discourses* plainly show. Anglo is right to claim that he is not in fact very consistent in this. Frequently it is evident that the generalization has come to his mind first, from whatever source, and that the historical examples are merely used as illustrations. But the interesting question is whether it could be better done.

Once this question is put, it is clear that a familiar problem of induction may be thought to arise. As Hume and countless others have pointed out, we cannot validly infer from any finite number of instances of one event being followed by another, that future occurrences of the first event must be followed by the second. Nowadays, the problem is mainly discussed in the context of natural science, but if it presents a real difficulty to theorizing about physical phenomena, it will present the same difficulty to induction from historical phenomena. Many philosophers, of course, have argued for a variety of solutions to the problem of induction, and even when these are not found to be convincing, others have argued that, for practical purposes, the same degree of logical rigour cannot be expected from inductive reasoning as deductive reasoning. No one denies, I think, that there can be practical rules of thumb or that these can be based, albeit somewhat loosely, on past instances. In short, for practical purposes we need generalizations; we do not need logically validated universalizations, and it is only in generalizations that Machiavelli and others have claimed to trade.

There is some reason, then, not to take up the problem of induction in its general form here. Either it has a solution, or it is not as devastating for practice as it is for theory. However, there is another problem for the inductive method which is more troublesome, and arguably more troublesome for a 'science of history' than for a natural science and which cannot be set aside in a similar fashion. Natural scientists, and philosophers who know something of natural science, are rarely really troubled by the problem of induction. That is to say, they recognize it as a deep and interesting conceptual issue, but do not seriously doubt the success or validity of natural science. In other words, like other philosophical problems, it is not regarded as genuinely troublesome, because firm intuition tells us that it must have some solution.

The same thing cannot be said for attempts to generalize from political history, since in this case there are widespread and genuine doubts about whether the events of human history can be treated in the same way as events in the natural world. Machiavelli does not share these doubts. In the passage quoted from the *Discourses* he explicitly draws a parallel between politics and medicine, and between the behaviour of states and the behaviour of the sun and the elements (by which he means fire, water and so on). He allows, of course, for who could deny, that the outward forms of human action change from period to period and from one cultural context to another. But he maintains that beneath this variety there is continuity; the passions and desires from which human actions spring remain the same.

Any one comparing the present with the past will soon perceive that in all cities and in all nations there prevail the same desires and passions as always have prevailed; for which reason it should be an easy matter for him who carefully examines past events, to foresee those which are about to happen in any republic, and to apply such remedies as the ancients have used in like cases. (*Discourses*, p. 29)

Machiavelli is here making an inference, the validity of which may be questioned. Let us agree that throughout the great variety of historical forms that human culture and society have taken, there is an underlying, common, human nature. Let us further suppose that this is composed in part of universal desires and passions. That is to say, men have fought different kinds of battles, using different instruments of war, for a variety of purposes, but what has driven all of them to war are such things as pride, love of kith and kin, religious loyalty, avarice, fear, hope of glory, and so on. Whether or not this is true, it does not follow that knowledge of these motives puts us in a position to predict actions and outcomes. To begin with, and this is the least interesting point, the motivations of human beings tend to be complex in a way that the behaviour of natural objects is not. The precise 'mix' of the passions in any human being or group of human beings is not as easily determined as the combination of physical properties in, say, a metal. To know then that all human beings are moved by love and fear (itself a simplification, though a favourite maxim of Machiavelli's) is not necessarily to know which will predominate from person to person or even from occasion to occasion in the same person. Of course, one might hope for ever more sophisticated generalizations which would accommodate something of this complexity. Machiavelli himself believed fear to be, almost invariably, a more powerful motive than love.

Machiavelli in fact grants that politics cannot be an exact science. Indeed, throughout several of his works he returns to a problem which he, rightly, regards as being of crucial importance to all his endeavours. "I think it astonishing to see some generals achieve by the very opposite course of conduct the same results that have been attained by those who have conformed to the rules we have recommended above" (*Discourses*, p. 473). And conversely, he is puzzled by the cases in which those who have followed the rules have been defeated. By way of resolving the difficulty, he introduces his celebrated distinction between *virtú* and *fortuna*. The explanation of things not going according to plan is the hand *fortuna*, or chance, takes in the disposition of affairs. Those who have the sort of ability and strength of will which constitutes *virtú* may overcome the vagaries of *fortuna*, but this is not always the case. Consequently, though the rules hold in general, the presence of *fortuna* ensures that they cannot be guaranteed success.

It is widely agreed by commentators that Machiavelli does not delineate the concepts of *virtú* and *fortuna* satisfactorily, but it is hard to resist the thought that in any case they are and could be nothing more than devices designed to bolster up the deficiencies in his theory. It does not take much reflection to uncover a deep-seated incoherence in his conception of action and prescription. If princes, generals and the like can learn from historical experience, so can those they aim to rule or conquer. But in this case, if the initiating action, being informed by history, can be different than it would otherwise be, so too can the response, with the result that the course of history does *not* follow that of its supposed precedents.

The general point which this possibility illustrates is that there is a further and more important difference between human actions and natural events than their relative complexity. Human actions are governed by intelligence; natural events are not. Despite the familiar analogy, battles are radically different from games of chess; soldiers are not pawns. Machiavelli invites us to compare politics with medicine. But the physiological processes of the body cannot respond differently to medication by learning that it is about to be applied, any more than fire can decide to hide itself underground at the approaching sound of the fire engine. The intelligence of human action calls into question a different aspect of the technique of inductive generalization than that with which the traditional problem of induction is concerned. This has to do with identifying instances of 'the same' phenomenon. We can universalize or generalize only over instances of the same phenomenon. In the case of natural phenomena 'sameness' is not a problem; one case of water running downhill is just like another from the point of view of understanding the physical processes at work and it does not matter when or where it took place. But when it comes to understanding human actions this is not true. Events in human history, unlike events in the natural world, can take place in the knowledge of one another, and hence time and place, which make these events unique, do matter. How then could it be possible to regard events in a properly historical sequence simply as repeated instances of the same thing?

This is a problem that has dogged the so-called social sciences when they have proceeded on the basis of inductive generalization. Suppose I aim to construct a theory of revolutions, not for the practical purposes of causing or containing them, but just in order to describe their normal course. An important obstacle in the way of doing so is the fact that the participants in one may be acting in the knowledge of an earlier one, and precisely because of this, the course of their revolution is different to those which preceded it. This has no parallel in natural phenomena. Though no doubt meteorological phenomena are causally connected, they are not connected by intelligence. One summer does not try to do better than the last.

Does this mean that the course of political history cannot be understood or explained? No. It means only that it cannot be explained by 'theories' employing inductive generalization. Nor, indeed, is the very idea of a social science in this sense ruled out. There may be phenomena that are not primarily the outcome of intelligent action, or at least not directly so—economic cycles might be an example—and perhaps it is reasonable to hope for law-like theories of these, even perhaps for mathematically expressible ones. But whatever the prospects of this, a large part of the study of human affairs, and politics is a prime example, cannot take this form.[1] What form can it take, then? One answer is 'narrative', and this brings us back to some of the themes of the last chapter.

II

The structure of narrative having been discussed already at some length, it is necessary only to offer a few reminders here. Narratives connect sequences of events by relating them in a story which

---

[1] An influential discussion of some of these points in relation to politics will be found in Alasdair MacIntyre's essay 'Is a science of comparative politics possible?' in *Against the Self-Images of the Age*, pp. 260–80.

has some controlling *telos*. While it is necessary for historical narratives to be built out of fact, factuality is not a sufficient condition of a successful narrative, which must also operate with a principle or principles picking out of the mass of facts those that are relevant to the *telos*. A narrative, whether historical or fictional, normally begins with origins, traces a development, reaches or anticipates a culmination and, sometimes, describes a denouement. This is precisely what Augustine aims to do. What marks out his narrative is its ambition—it aspires to be a narrative of the whole of history—and the religious nature of its *telos*: God's saving work. But there is another distinguishing aim also: its practical relevance. This is a feature that it shares with the histories of Machiavelli and other practical historians, but what is noteworthy for present purposes is the rather different way in which this third task is attempted. It is the exploration of this alternative conception of practical relevance, in fact, which will allow us to take stock of the various shapes of the past recounted.

What is the general point of writing narratives? The answer differs according to whether it is fictional or historical narrative we have in mind. In the case of fiction we might summarize the point as either entertainment or edification.[2] The point of historical narratives, again broadly speaking, is the provision of knowledge and understanding. Such knowledge and understanding may have no purpose other than itself, but it may also be sought from the point of view of action. One alternative to the confused approach of Machiavelli, and possibly the only one, is to seek practical relevance, not in the form of general principles of action, but in a narrative which is personal. That is to say, I might set out to find a history which is *my* history. The personal in this

---

[2] This is a very bald summary of what I think to be the most plausible conclusion to be drawn from extended arguments in aesthetics. I deal with these at length in *Aesthetics and Experience* (New York, Paragon Press, 1997).

sense need not be individualistic, however. We can seek a narrative which is *our* history, and the collectivity which the 'our' refers to can have greater or lesser extension. In the case of the Old Testament it is the history of the Jewish people for Jews. This may be presented as the history of an ethnic or national grouping, albeit one which has a kind of inherent universalism. Personal histories of such groupings have proved perennially attractive. Human beings, for good or ill, seem naturally to think of themselves in terms of races, peoples, and nations, and to seek and write histories accordingly. But it is not difficult to find similar histories of smaller collectivities—families, sects, professions, clans for instance. In contrast to these, world histories, philosophical histories, universal histories, sacred histories—the different labels do not signify here—are attempts to write a narrative in which we regard ourselves simply as human beings. The practical concern is not diminished in this, however. The oracle at Delphi's ancient injunction—"Man, know thyself"—is exhibited here just as plainly as in less ambitious projects, and what is sought is a narrative understanding of the past that will satisfy the age-old desire to know not merely what human existence and experience has been, or even what it has arisen from, but what it signifies.

I have already argued that those who are sceptical about the possibility of a philosophical or universal history on the grounds that it brings evaluative conceptions to bear upon a past which, in history proper, should be allowed to speak for itself, do not have good grounds for this restriction; and further that the philosophical examination of the evaluative concepts which are brought to bear in this way is a respectable endeavour. But the refutation of this one ground of objection, does not put paid to all sceptical doubts about the validity of the enterprise. We might still wonder whether, even if it is coherent, universal history is not too ambitious ever to be completed satisfactorily and, relatedly, whether the competing claims of the many contenders might not have rendered it impossible to arrive at even qualified, provisional conclusions. Let us consider each of these doubts in turn, beginning with the second.

Five shapes of the past have been examined. Can the conclusions of the chapters devoted to each of these be welded together in anything like a coherent form? The problem with recurrence theories was this: whichever analogy we employ to describe the structure they purport to detect—whether that of seasonal variation, or that of the life of an organism—a division has to be made between ages or cultures or civilizations such that each is distinct. According to all such theories, each civilization begins, develops, declines, and finally disappears. But we saw the implausibility of drawing sharp divisions between ages or cultures. The ancient, mediaeval and modern European worlds, for example, certainly have deep differences, but there are deep continuities as well. We may now offer a partial explanation of these continuities. It lies with the intelligent character of human action and creativity which marks out human endeavour. The culture of Europe in the modern and mediaeval periods has in part been what it has been because of a knowledge and understanding of the ancients. Some examples of this are specially striking. The intellectual high point of mediaeval Christendom is the hugely influential theology and metaphysics of St Thomas Aquinas (1225–74). But Aquinas's achievement is fairly summarized as the unification of biblical religion with Aristotelian philosophy. What brought the dominance of mediaeval Christendom to an end was in part another rediscovery of the ancient world, at the time of the Renaissance. Yet the religious Reformation which the Renaissance did much to promote, in its turn induced something of a revival of the mediaeval theology of heaven and hell. And so on.

What this sort of example illustrates, and there are similar cases in other civilizations, is that even where meaningful distinctions can be drawn between cultures, the fact that many aspects of a later culture have been formed in the knowledge and light of earlier ones determines a relationship of accumulation and not merely succession between them. It is this relationship of accumulation which creates a real prospect of universal or world history. Critics and sceptics have been right to point to the constant twofold danger of over-generalization and windy abstraction when anyone undertakes to offer us a *universal* history. Nevertheless, as culture succeeds culture, and each succeeding culture is able to see itself not merely as successor but inheritor, it becomes part of a continuing narrative of a developing human civilization. This is true also where radically different cultures meet. The confrontation of the 'civilized' Old World with the 'savage' New, was not an uncomprehending encounter of aliens, but a protracted event which caused a re-evaluation in the self-understanding of both.

The question arises as to the proper construction that is to be put upon such developments. To call them 'developments' may be thought to prejudge this issue in favour of some sort of progressivism, but while it is true that a wholly neutral word is hard to find, the development of one culture out of another allows in principle for degeneration and eventual collapse as much as for progressive development. Both these competing suggestions were examined in previous chapters. It emerged that a theory of decline as a 'shape' of universal history is not strictly an alternative to progressive theories. Even with respect to its most plausible prima-facie case, religion, it is hard to substantiate empirically, and in this and similar instances, it overlooks the possibility of the sort of transformation to which Hegel gives the name *Aufhebung*. So too with theories of cultural collapse. Though there are, no doubt, instances of periodic decline and local political collapse, it is impossible to sustain a concept of total cultural extinction or disruption. Even in a world as deeply riven as that of England during the Civil Wars, there will be fundamental beliefs, conceptions and concerns which underlie the very sources of strife and division themselves. And whole worlds that have hitherto lived in ignorance of each other will, upon meeting, eventually find common ground.

Of the candidates considered, then, only progress and providence have emerged, so far, relatively unscathed. What we now need to ask is whether these are in fact rivals, or whether each is made more plausible in so far as they are held to be complementary.

I argued earlier that human progress is not best understood as a steady encyclopaedic accumulation, but as a series of Hegelian transformations in which earlier forms are both preserved and transcended in later ones. It is this transformative conception which best accommodates both difference and continuity. The plainest example of progress so conceived is scientific and technological change. The problem was whether a similar conception could be extended to other aspects of culture such as art, morality, religion, and politics. These, it was held, were more obvious candidates for decline, collapse, or recurrence. But now that we have uncovered quite general deficiencies in the alternatives, it is time to consider again whether Hegelian progress can accommodate them.

One way of approaching this question is to inquire further into the *telos* which any concept of progress must employ. Progress is not merely change, or even development, but development to the greater realization of a good end. On the Aristotelian conception of progress this end is given by human nature and the 'good for man'. But this static conception of the *telos* fails to account for a development in the understanding of the good for man itself. Human nature, once we depart from basic biological requirements, is not in fact fixed, as perhaps the nature of other creatures largely is. This is not to say that it is wholly fluid. The best forms of human association and activity are discovered rather than invented in the sense that there are constraints, including both those of logic and the human condition, on how human beings may understand themselves and hence may live. This is a thought to which Augustine, in keeping with certain fundamental elements in Christian theology, gives great importance. The whole creation, in the image of St Paul, "groaneth and travaileth", and human nature itself is undergoing a process of transformation, in theological language a process of redemption. This conception of progress as transformation implies that the *telos* of civilization does not consist in first principles from which learning proceeds, but the striving for an end whose intelligibility arises from a source with which the mind better conforms as it is itself changed. Progress on this conception will still be exhibited empirically in such things as improved understanding, more advanced technology, better social and political forms. Adequately understanding its character as progress, however, requires the postulation of a larger context of value and intelligibility of which at any given stage we have only a partial if improving grasp.

The inclusion of social and political forms in this brief list of empirically exhibited development may do something to accommodate the idea of moral progress within a more general historical thesis. Plausible examples of moral progress include the slow but eventual elimination of slavery, and more importantly the end of its acceptance or approval. Even if slavery continues to exist, it is hidden, and no one now could argue in its favour and expect to win serious attention. Barbaric forms of torture and punishment are no longer publicly acceptable, and this is partly the result of more refined and sophisticated conceptions of justice. Certainly, people continue to be victims of such treatment, though in smaller numbers than in the past, but in every part of the world accusations of torture and barbarity are strenuously denied, even by those who in effect condone or practice them, and their hypocrisy, if that is what it is, is in itself evidence of moral progress. In a similar fashion, as Fukuyama observes, individual equality and liberal democratic institutions are widely heralded as the only acceptable forms of political association, even if they are very imperfectly realized in most places. There are very many tyrannical regimes, but almost none that are self-confessedly illiberal and undemocratic. It is true that all these are instances of what are fragile accomplishments in many parts of the modern world. Moreover, they have been constantly under threat in this century. Nevertheless, there is good reason to regard them as evidence of progress. It is not just that the perpetrators of the Holocaust have been defeated, but that those in whom a certain sympathy with them lingers must now, so to speak, utter their sentiments *sotto voce*.

To believe in progress, moral or otherwise, is to pass clear judgement on cultures, ancient or modern, in which features regarded as progressive are absent or resented. This makes progressivism an unwelcome thesis in many quarters because it is so contrary to the spirit of relativism which pervades modern thought. Yet the modern 'liberal' world, though it inclines strongly to relativism, also believes in toleration, which is to say that it regards moral, religious, and political toleration as a virtue. It also believes, by and large, that the emergence of toleration as an historically widespread phenomenon is a commendable achievement. At the same time, it distances itself from the robust belief in moral progress typical of the nineteenth century. Indeed, part of the modern ideal of toleration is precisely held to be a willingness to abandon the nineteenth-century idea that some cultures are better than others because they are more developed or represent a higher stage of civilization.

It is not difficult to see that there is the makings of a contradiction here. If the emergence of toleration is a welcome development in human history, this must represent a measure of moral progress. Therefore, it would seem, those societies in which it has emerged have, to this degree at least, progressed beyond those in which it has not, and for that reason are to be preferred. Yet this, it seems, is the sort of judgement which the modern ideal of toleration forbids us to make. How is this contradiction to be resolved? The answer is that it is not. Modern relativists rarely, if ever, speak in favour of child sacrifice, trial by ordeal, or female circumcision. Though they preach the merits of cultural relativism, they do not actually regard all cultural practices as equally good, and this strengthens the conclusion that the existence of moral progress over time is a point with which most people do in fact concur.

What is much less obvious is whether culture in the narrower sense of art, music, literature and so on, can also be accommodated within this general conception of progress or whether with respect to these the relativist's position is more persuasive. In the case of culture narrowly conceived, to construe history as a series of discrete episodes which may or may not have a recurrent structure seems much more plausible. Even here, however, three points in favour of a progressivist interpretation of the past are worth making. First, the arts are not immune to progressive developments. The mastery of perspective and foreshortening in pictorial representation counts as progress because it secures better one aim of representation—the creation of resemblance— and because it is an attainment which later art, however it may use or neglect it, cannot undo. There are similar developments in other arts—harmonic forms and better instruments in music, engineering techniques in architecture. Second, there is an historical relationship of intelligent accumulation in the arts as much as in other aspects of culture. Later forms are what they are partly in virtue of their knowledge of earlier forms and contemporary artists see themselves as inheritors of an artworld whose aspirations and standards are the products of its history.

The third point relevant to progress and the arts is somewhat different. The degree to which culture in the narrow sense has to be accommodated in an account of universal progress for that progress to be correctly thought of as progress overall may be limited. It depends upon what the *telos* of human progress is thought to be. If the universal history with which we are concerned is a

sacred history, and if we follow Augustine, art will be an important element only in so far as it plays a part in salvation history.
Given the close association of the arts with the Christian religion, it would in fact be hard for a Christian sacred historian to
deny them a significant place, but the more general point is that
not everything which counts as culture needs to be accommodated into a universal history of progress. If, for instance, it could
be shown that the histories of science, technology, morality, politics, and the arts all exhibited progress in significant degrees,
and that this progress could be construed as a gradual realization of some larger end, it would not count as much of a defect
that sports and games, which have played a prominent part in
many cultures, could not be given a progressive structure.

So too with the arts, perhaps. The author of a sacred history
can plausibly make out a case without including the arts among
those things "needful to salvation", and a non-sacred universal
history might give them a relatively minor role in the process of
civilization. Fukuyama, for instance, is a progressivist who has
little to say about culture in the narrow sense and whatever the
defects in his account of the past, it is not any the less a universal history for that.

III

If the line of argument I have been pursuing is correct, and
progress as the shape of the past overcomes conceptual difficulties better than its rivals while at the same time having a reasonable empirical basis, three questions remain. Does it satisfy
the requirement of practical relevance? Does it need to be a *universal* history? And does it further imply a sacred history?

To answer the first of these questions it is useful to return
briefly to the example of the soldier in war. To make his place in
a war both intelligible and satisfactory, a soldier needs to fashion a narrative conception of what is happening and how it has

come about in which his actions and efforts, his emotions and attitudes, and his factual and moral beliefs are adequately accommodated. This is what will make a given story of the war *his* story. 'Accommodation' here means that within the narrative all these elements cohere; his pride or his fear, say, is not misplaced because of false beliefs or erroneous evaluations. Coherence of this sort, of course, leaves scope for a wide variety of *kinds* of story. It is not necessary, for instance, that the end result must be a conception in which the soldier's heart and soul are given to 'the cause'. It is necessary only that his attitudes, beliefs and so on should not be in conflict. This requirement is just as compatible with his thinking that he has been thrown by circumstances into a world of evils and chaos, as it is with a perception of himself as engaged in a Christian crusade.

When a soldier possesses this kind of understanding of his agency and circumstances, his world and its past has (some) meaning for him. To this degree the world becomes his home, and this is something more than a metaphor here. To make a home for oneself in the narrow sense is to order one's environment from a practical point of view, not just for the purposes of more efficient shelter, nutrition, and procreation, but with an eye to comfort and familiarity. In a similar way, to locate my experience in a narrative of past and present gives it meaning in a way that makes the world my home.

The first question, then, has a clear, and positive, answer; to arrive at an adequate personal history is to come to possess a practical understanding of experience, one, that is to say, whose principal significance is to allow us to live. This practical relevance lies in its being reflectively evaluative, rather than predictively prescriptive in the way Machiavelli seeks. It does not provide us with techniques that will enable us to manipulate the world more effectively to the securing of preconceived desires or ends such as food and shelter. Rather it makes our own agency intelligible to us.

One striking feature of this sort of understanding is that it has no determinate end; it inevitably reaches wider and wider. Even the relatively simple case of the soldier illustrates this. He begins with a need to understand his immediate circumstances—his position and orders, for instance—but to do so he must understand the significance of the battle, and then the campaign, the war, the context of its occurrence, and so on. Of course, to say that the pursuit of intelligibility has no end is not to say that those who pursue it never stop, and different people will stop at different points. One soldier may be satisfied if he can understand the point of this particular battle, another may require explanation of the politics behind the war. Yet others may proceed to ideas of war and violence and on from this conceptions of death or justice, and so on.

Here we find a pattern, in fact, which was also to be found in a much earlier example—that of psychiatry. A psychiatrist might take stock of his activity, and ask what his work amounts to. It is natural to pursue this question beyond personal, countable, achievements—patients cured, papers written—important though these may be, and into the realms of the history of psychiatry and the aims of the practice itself, and, as I argued earlier, it is inevitable that this in turn raises questions about the nature and value of science, the nature and value of healing, the character of mind and hence of the psychiatrist's own mind. Of course psychiatrists no less than soldiers can be relatively unreflective, but the general point is that to pursue a personal history in this sense is to be launched upon a trajectory, to be led into ever wider and wider connections, reflections, and speculations. Michael Oakeshott has described this dialectical movement with characteristic depth of thought and beauty of style.

The reflective intelligence is apt to find itself at this level without the consciousness of any great conversion and without any sense of entering upon a new project, but merely by submitting itself to the impetus of reflection, by spreading its sails to the argument. For, any man who holds in his mind the conceptions of the natural world, of God, of human activity and human destiny which belong to his civilization, will scarely be able to prevent an endeavour to assimilate these to the political order in which he lives, and failing to do so he will become a philosopher (of a simple sort) unawares. (*Introduction to Hobbes*, p. ix)

In this feature of human understanding, we encounter something comparable to the expanding hermeneutic circle discussed before. Indeed the two sorts of expansion are complementary —as the methods of the understanding increase, so does its content, and vice versa. For the activity of the mind and of the resources it employs, there is arguably no outer limit. The pursuit of an intelligible narrative, unlike more simple ascertainments of fact, is best characterized by its intellectual ambition. In this sense universal history is implicit in it; to seek to understand oneself is, in the end, to seek to understand the human condition and the purposes of human existence.

It is true, certainly, that this ambition can remain unfulfilled. This might be because any given intellect which undertakes it, or has done to date, is inadequate to the task. But from the fact that minds with the breadth of Hegel's seem to fail, there is reason to suppose that failure is inherent to the ambition. If so, what are we to make of this? It does not seem reasonable to refuse ever to set out. For one thing, the belief upon which this would rest— that the pursuit of intelligibility can never be completed—is itself an understanding of what it is to be a human being. For another, the fact, if it is one, that the perfect must elude us, does not eliminate the value of the imperfect. But more than this, we know that between us and other animals there is what we might call a cognitive chain. Dogs and chimpanzees have some measure of intelligence by which they learn from experience. They may even be said to know—people and places, for instance. We are higher in the chain because we, unlike them, can know something of the basis of their knowledge, and we have the powers of mind which so impressed Hobbes—recall and imagination. But as John Searle has pointed out (in *The Rediscovery of the Mind*), there is an unwarranted assumption in contemporary epistemology that we are at the end of the chain, that there is nothing objectively true which we cannot come to know. Might it not be that there are higher beings of whose nature and existence we can know as little as a dog can know of the existence of the human mind?

This brings us to the third and final question: why move from universal history to sacred history? One recent writer, discussing the inadequacies of contemporary metaphysics and epistemology, has urged this move in what is perhaps its strongest form:

That the attainment of truth in human minds should proceed as Aquinas says "through certain doors" (*Scriptum super libros sententiarium*, III, d. 35, q. 2, a. 2) is a mystery that is explored, though not wholly explained, by the sacred history presented in Holy Writ. Odd indeed as it sounds, my conclusion is that those in search of understanding knowledge might consider periodically setting aside epistemological texts and turning to Scripture. (Haldane, p. 183)

This close connection between the concerns of epistemologists and the books of the Bible may or may not be sustainable. But there is a weaker form in which something of the same move is to be recommended, and perhaps more plausibly. In seeking to understand the character of ourselves as human beings we have to take account of the existence of religion. One way of doing so is through religious phenomenology. That is to say, we can seek to record and recount the religious in human life without entering the question of its epistemological value or significance. But to put a block upon our understanding of religion in this way is to put an arbitrary limit on the pursuit of understanding. The pursuit of understanding proper is, to quote Oakeshott again, "without qualification or arrest" (*Experience and its Modes*, p. 2). As he says in the same place, for philosophy, by which he means the sort of understanding I have been describing, nothing is mere error; everything has its place in an adequate understanding if only we can find it. And this includes the repositories of religion, their devotional practices and their sacred texts. Moreover, if what I began by calling philosophical history is intelligible, and if it begins and ends in ideas of value and significance, it is most likely to succeed if it draws upon the source or sources in which human beings have, albeit dimly, repeatedly and continuously thought that the greatest significance and value lie.

Bibliography

ANGLO, S., *Machiavelli* (London, Paladin, 1971).

ANSCOMBE, G. E. M., 'Modern Moral Philosophy' in *Collected Essays*, iii (Oxford, Blackwell, 1981).

ARNOLD, M., 'Literature and Dogma' in *The Complete Works of Matthew Arnold*, vi (Ann Arbor, Michigan University Press, 1968).

AUGUSTINE, *City of God*, trans. H. Bettenson, ed. D. Knowles (Harmondsworth, Penguin Classics, 1972).

BARNARD, F. M., *Herder's Social and Political Thought* (Oxford, Clarendon Press, 1965).

BEISER, F. C., 'Hegel's historicism' in *The Cambridge Companion to Hegel*, ed. F. C. Beiser (Cambridge, Cambridge University Press, 1993).

Bible: *Revised English Bible* (Oxford, Oxford University Press, 1989).

BOLINGBROKE, *On the Study and Use of History* in *The Works of Lord Bolingbroke*, ii. 173–334 (London, Frank Cass, 1967).

—— *The Idea of a Patriot King* in *The Works of Lord Bolingbroke*, ii. 372–430 (London, Frank Cass, 1967).

BUNYAN, J., *Grace Abounding to the Chief of Sinners* (Oxford, Oxford University Press, 1966).

BUTTERFIELD, H., *Writings on Christianity and History*, ed. C. T. McIntyre (New York, Oxford University Press, 1979).

CUPITT, DON, *Taking Leave of God* (London, SCM Press, 1980).

DRETSKE, F. I., *Knowledge and the Flow of Information* (Oxford, Blackwell, 1981).

ENGELS, F., *State of the Working-class in England in 1844*, trans. Wischnewetsky (St Albans, Panther, 1969).

FEUERBACH, L., *The Essence of Christianity*, trans. George Eliot (New York, Harper and Row, 1957).

FEYERABEND, P., *Against Method* (3rd edn.) (New York, Verso, 1993).

FODOR, J., *The Language of Thought* (Hassocks, Harvester Press, 1976).

FRAZER, Sir J. G., *The Golden Bough* (London, Macmillan, 1913).

FUKUYAMA, F., *The End of History and the Last Man* (London, Hamish Hamilton, 1992).

GALLIE, W. B., 'Essentially Contested Concepts', *Proceedings of the Aristotelian Society*, 56 (1956), 167–98.

GIBBARD, A., *Wise Choices, Apt Feelings* (Oxford, Clarendon Press, 1990).

HALDANE, J., 'Reason, Truth and Sacred History', *American Catholic Philosophical Quarterly*, 68 (1994).

HEGEL, G. W. F., *The Philosophy of Right*, trans. T. M. Knox (Oxford, Clarendon Press, 1942).

—— *Lectures on the Philosophy of World History*, trans. H. B. Nisbet (Cambridge, Cambridge University Press, 1975).

HERDER, J. G., *Reflections on the Philosophy of the History of Mankind*, trans. T. O. Churchill (London, University of Chicago Press, 1968).

HILL, C., *A Turbulent, Seditious, and Factious People* (Oxford, Oxford University Press, 1989).

HUME, D., *The Natural History of Religion* (Oxford, Clarendon Press, 1976).

—— *Of Miracles* (La Salle, Ill., Open Court, 1985).

INWOOD, M., *A Hegel Dictionary* (Oxford, Blackwell, 1992).

JAMES, W., *The Will to Believe*, ed. F. H. Burkhardt (Cambridge, Mass., Harvard University Press, 1979).

KANT, I., *Critique of Practical Reason*, trans. T. K. Abbot (London, Longmans, 1927).

—— *Critique of Pure Reason*, trans. N. K. Smith (London, Macmillan, 1929).

—— *Critique of Judgement*, trans. W. S. Pluhar (Indianapolis, Hackett, 1987).

—— *The Idea of a Universal History from a Cosmopolitan Point of View*, trans. L. W. Beck in L. W. Beck (ed.), *On History*, pp. 11–27 (Indianapolis, Library of Liberal Arts, 1963).

LUCRETIUS, *De Rerum Natura*, Loeb Classical Library (London, Harvard University Press, repr. 1992).

MACHIAVELLI, N., *Discourses on the First Decade of Titus Livius*, trans. N. H. Thomson (London, Routledge & Kegan Paul, 1950).

—— *The Prince*, trans. Luigi Ricci (Oxford, World's Classics, 1935).

MacIntyre, A., *Secularization and Moral Change* (Oxford, Clarendon Press, 1967).

—— *Against the Self Images of the Age* (London, Gerald Duckworth, 1971).

—— *After Virtue* (2nd edn.) (Notre Dame, Ind., Notre Dame University Press, 1984).

—— *Whose Justice, Which Rationality?* (London, Gerald Duckworth, 1988).

—— *Three Rival Versions of Moral Inquiry* (London, Gerald Duckworth, 1990).

McPherson, J. M., *Battle Cry of Freedom* (New York, Oxford University Press, 1988).

Marx, K., *Capital*, trans. D. Fernbach (Harmondsworth, Penguin, 1981).

Marx, K. and Engels, F., *The Communist Manifesto*, trans. D. Moore (Harmondsworth, Penguin, 1967).

Midgley, M., *Beast and Man* (Hassocks, Harvester Press, 1978).

Nietzsche, F., *On the Genealogy of Morality* (ed. K. Ansell-Pearson, trans. C. Diethe) (New York, Cambridge University Press, 1994).

Oakeshott, M., *Experience and its Modes* (Cambridge, Cambridge University Press, 1933 reprinted 1966).

—— Introduction to Hobbes' *Leviathan* (Oxford, Blackwell, 1960).

—— *On Human Conduct* (Oxford, Clarendon Press, 1975).

Pellegrino, C., *Return to Sodom and Gomorrah* (New York, Random House, 1994).

Pompa, L., (ed. and trans.) *Vico: Selected Writings* (Cambridge, Cambridge University Press, 1982).

Plato, *Republic*, Loeb Classical Library (London, Harvard University Press, repr. 1994).

—— *Meno*, Loeb Classical Library (London, Harvard University Press, repr. 1990).

Popper, K., *The Open Society and its Enemies* (5th edn.) (London, Routledge & Kegan Paul, 1966).

—— *The Poverty of Historicism* (London, Routledge & Kegan Paul, 1957).

Robinson, J., *Honest to God* (London, SCM Press, 1963).

Rorty, R., *Philosophy and the Mirror of Nature* (Princeton, Princeton University Press, 1979).

ROUSSEAU, J-J., *On the Social Contract*, ed. and trans. Donald A. Cress (Indianapolis, Hackett, 1983).

SCHLEIERMACHER, F., *On Religion: Speeches to its Cultured Despisers*, trans. J. Oman (New York, Harper & Row, 1958).

SEARLE, J., *The Rediscovery of the Mind* (Cambridge, Mass., MIT Press, 1994).

SKINNER, Q., 'Who are "We"?: Ambiguities of the Modern Self', *Inquiry*, 34 (1991).

SMITH, C. W., *The Reason Why* (London, Constable, 1953).

SPENGLER, O., *The Decline of the West* (1 vol.) trans. C. F. Atkinson (London, George Allen & Unwin, 1926).

TAYLOR, C., *Sources of the Self* (Cambridge, Mass., Harvard University Press, 1989).

THOMAS, K., *Religion and the Decline of Magic* (Harmondsworth, Penguin, 1978).

TILLICH, P., *The Courage to Be* (London, Fontana, 1968).

TOYNBEE, A., *Study of History* (Oxford, Oxford University Press, 1972).

VICO, G., *The New Science of Giambattista Vico*, trans. T. G. Bergin and M. M. Fisch (Ithaca, NY, Cornell University Press, 1984).

Index

OXFORD

MORE OXFORD PAPERBACKS

This book is just one of nearly 1000 Oxford Paperbacks currently in print. If you would like details of other Oxford Paperbacks, including titles in the World's Classics, Oxford Reference, Oxford Books, OPUS, Past Masters, Oxford Authors, and Oxford Shakespeare series, please write to:

UK and Europe: Oxford Paperbacks Publicity Manager, Arts and Reference Publicity Department, Oxford University Press, Walton Street, Oxford OX2 6DP.

Customers in UK and Europe will find Oxford Paperbacks available in all good bookshops. But in case of difficulty please send orders to the Cash-with-Order Department, Oxford University Press Distribution Services, Saxon Way West, Corby, Northants NN18 9ES. Tel: 01536 741519; Fax: 01536 746337. Please send a cheque for the total cost of the books, plus £1.75 postage and packing for orders under £20; £2.75 for orders over £20. Customers outside the UK should add 10% of the cost of the books for postage and packing.

USA: Oxford Paperbacks Marketing Manager, Oxford University Press, Inc., 200 Madison Avenue, New York, N.Y. 10016.

Canada: Trade Department, Oxford University Press, 70 Wynford Drive, Don Mills, Ontario M3C 1J9.

Australia: Trade Marketing Manager, Oxford University Press, G.P.O. Box 2784Y, Melbourne 3001, Victoria.

South Africa: Oxford University Press, P.O. Box 1141, Cape Town 8000.

PHILOSOPHY IN OXFORD PAPERBACKS
THE GREAT PHILOSOPHERS

Bryan Magee

Beginning with the death of Socrates in 399, and following the story through the centuries to recent figures such as Bertrand Russell and Wittgenstein, Bryan Magee and fifteen contemporary writers and philosophers provide an accessible and exciting introduction to Western philosophy and its greatest thinkers.

Bryan Magee in conversation with:

A. J. Ayer
Michael Ayers
Miles Burnyeat
Frederick Copleston
Hubert Dreyfus
Anthony Kenny
Sidney Morgenbesser
Martha Nussbaum

John Passmore
Anthony Quinton
John Searle
Peter Singer
J. P. Stern
Geoffrey Warnock
Bernard Williams

'Magee is to be congratulated . . . anyone who sees the programmes or reads the book will be left in no danger of believing philosophical thinking is unpractical and uninteresting.' Ronald Hayman, *Times Educational Supplement*

'one of the liveliest, fast-paced introductions to philosophy, ancient and modern that one could wish for' *Universe*

OPUS

A HISTORICAL INTRODUCTION TO THE PHILOSOPHY OF SCIENCE

John Losee

This challenging introduction, designed for readers without an extensive knowledge of formal logic or of the history of science, looks at the long-argued questions raised by philosophers and scientists about the proper evaluation of scientific interpretations. It offers an historical exposition of differing views on issues such as the merits of competing theories; the interdependence of observation and theory; and the nature of scientific progress. The author looks at explanations given by Plato, Aristotle, and Pythagoras, and through to Bacon and Descartes, to Nagel, Kuhn, and Laudan.

This edition incorporates an extended discussion of contemporary developments and changes within the history of science, and examines recent controversies and the search for a non-prescriptive philosophy of science.

'a challenging interdisciplinary work'
New Scientist

OPUS

TWENTIETH-CENTURY FRENCH PHILOSOPHY

Eric Matthews

This book gives a chronological survey of the works of the major French philosophers of the twentieth century.

Eric Matthews offers various explanations for the enduring importance of philosophy in French intellectual life and traces the developments which French philosophy has taken in the twentieth century from its roots in the thought of Descartes, with examinations of key figures such as Bergson, Sartre, Marcel, Merleau-Ponty, Foucault, and Derrida, and the recent French Feminists.

'*Twentieth-Century French Philosophy* is a clear, yet critical introduction to contemporary French Philosophy. . . . The undergraduate or other reader who comes to the area for the first time will gain a definite sense of an intellectual movement with its own questions and answers and its own rigour . . . not least of the book's virtues is its clarity.'
Garrett Barden
Author of *After Principles*

PHILOSOPHY IN OXFORD PAPERBACKS
THE GREAT PHILOSOPHERS

Bryan Magee

Beginning with the death of Socrates in 399, and following the story through the centuries to recent figures such as Bertrand Russell and Wittgenstein, Bryan Magee and fifteen contemporary writers and philosophers provide an accessible and exciting introduction to Western philosophy and its greatest thinkers.

Bryan Magee in conversation with:

A. J. Ayer	John Passmore
Michael Ayers	Anthony Quinton
Miles Burnyeat	John Searle
Frederick Copleston	Peter Singer
Hubert Dreyfus	J. P. Stern
Anthony Kenny	Geoffrey Warnock
Sidney Morgenbesser	Bernard Williams
Martha Nussbaum	

'Magee is to be congratulated . . . anyone who sees the programmes or reads the book will be left in no danger of believing philosophical thinking is unpractical and uninteresting.' Ronald Hayman, *Times Educational Supplement*

'one of the liveliest, fast-paced introductions to philosophy, ancient and modern that one could wish for' *Universe*

OXFORD

RETHINKING LIFE AND DEATH
THE COLLAPSE OF OUR TRADITIONAL ETHICS

Peter Singer

A victim of the Hillsborough Disaster in 1989, Anthony Bland lay in hospital in a coma being fed liquid food by a pump, via a tube passing through his nose and into his stomach. On 4 February 1993 Britain's highest court ruled that doctors attending him could lawfully act to end his life.

Our traditional ways of thinking about life and death are collapsing. In a world of respirators and embryos stored for years in liquid nitrogen, we can no longer take the sanctity of human life as the cornerstone of our ethical outlook.

In this controversial book Peter Singer argues that we cannot deal with the crucial issues of death, abortion, euthanasia and the rights of nonhuman animals unless we sweep away the old ethic and build something new in its place.

Singer outlines a new set of commandments, based on compassion and commonsense, for the decisions everyone must make about life and death.

PAST
MASTERS

PAST MASTERS

A wide range of unique, short, clear introductions to the lives and work of the world's most influential thinkers. Written by experts, they cover the history of ideas from Aristotle to Wittgenstein. Readers need no previous knowledge of the subject, so they are ideal for students and general readers alike.

Each book takes as its main focus the thought and work of its subject. There is a short section on the life and a final chapter on the legacy and influence of the thinker. A section of further reading helps in further research.

The series continues to grow, and future Past Masters will include **Owen Gingerich** on *Copernicus*, **R G Frey** on *Joseph Butler*, **Bhiku Parekh** on *Gandhi*, **Christopher Taylor** on *Socrates*, **Michael Inwood** on *Heidegger*, and **Peter Ghosh** on *Weber*.

MASTERS

KEYNES

Robert Skidelsky

John Maynard Keynes is a central thinker of the twentieth century. This is the only available short introduction to his life and work.

Keynes's doctrines continue to inspire strong feelings in admirers and detractors alike. This short, engaging study of his life and thought explores the many positive and negative stereotypes and also examines the quality of Keynes's mind, his cultural and social milieu, his ethical and practical philosophy, and his monetary thought. Recent scholarship has significantly altered the treatment and assessment of Keynes's contribution to twentieth-century economic thinking, and the current state of the debate initiated by the Keynesian revolution is discussed in a final chapter on its legacy.

MASTERS

RUSSELL

A. C. *Grayling*

Bertrand Russell (1872–1970) is one of the most famous and important philosophers of the twentieth century. In this account of his life and work A. C. Grayling introduces both his technical contributions to logic and philosophy, and his wide-ranging views on education, politics, war, and sexual morality. Russell is credited with being one of the prime movers of Analytic Philosophy, and with having played a part in the revolution in social attitudes witnessed throughout the twentieth-century world. This introduction gives a clear survey of Russell's achievements across their whole range.

THE OXFORD DICTIONARY OF PHILOSOPHY

Edited by Simon Blackburn

* 2,500 entries covering the entire span of the subject including the most recent terms and concepts

* Biographical entries for nearly 500 philosophers

* Chronology of philosophical events

From Aristotle to Zen, this is the most comprehensive, authoritative, and up to date dictionary of philosophy available. Ideal for students or a general readership, it provides lively and accessible coverage of not only the Western philosophical tradition but also important themes from Chinese, Indian, Islamic, and Jewish philosophy. The paperback includes a new Chronology.

'an excellent source book and can be strongly recommended . . . there are generous and informative entries on the great philosophers . . . Overall the entries are written in an informed and judicious manner.'
Times Higher Education Supplement